Dragon Boat Culture of Foshan China

中国佛山龙舟文化

佛山历史文化丛书·龙舟

李小艳 著　许勉君 译

广州新华出版发行集团
广州出版社

图书在版编目（CIP）数据

中国佛山龙舟文化 / 李小艳著；许勉君译. —广州：广州出版社，2020.10
（佛山历史文化丛书）
ISBN 978-7-5462-3099-3

Ⅰ.①中… Ⅱ.①李… ②许… Ⅲ.①龙舟竞赛—文化—佛山—汉、英 Ⅳ.①G852.9

中国版本图书馆CIP数据核字（2020）第149457号

书　　名　中国佛山龙舟文化
Zhongguo Foshan Longzhou Wenhua
出版发行　广州出版社
（地址：广州市天河区天润路87号9楼、10楼　邮政编码：510635
网址：www.gzcbs.com.cn）
出 版 人　柳宗慧
策　　划　佛山日报社
责任编辑　蚁燕娟　叶桂莲
文字编辑　李畅炜
责任校对　刘雅丽
责任技编　刘雁明
装帧设计　紫上视觉 刁俊锋+黄隽琳
题　　字　庞国钟
插　　画　黄珂展
印刷单位　广州市赢彩彩印有限公司
（地址：广州市白云区嘉禾鹤边鹤泰东路工业区C栋自编6号　邮政编码：511440）
规　　格　889毫米×1194毫米　1/32
字　　数　168千
印　　张　7.25
版　　次　2020年10月第1版
印　　次　2020年10月第1次
书　　号　ISBN 978-7-5462-3099-3
定　　价　56.00元

“佛山历史文化丛书”
编辑委员会
Foshan History and Culture Series Editorial Board

目 录

CONTENTS

中国佛山 龙舟文化

Dragon Boat Culture of Foshan China

FOSHAN

第一章 佛山龙舟源远流长

Chapter 1 A Long History of Foshan Dragon Boats

中国广东佛山自古以来就是滨海之地，境内沼泽密布、水网众多，水神崇拜风气盛行。龙是佛山人重要的水神，龙舟就是龙的化身，人们扒龙船（划龙舟、扒龙舟）祭祀水神龙，以求得风调雨顺、五谷丰登。扒龙舟深受佛山民众喜爱，明清时期端午划龙舟，村村皆然。进入21世纪，扒龙舟开展得如火如荼，佛山也成为“中国龙舟龙狮运动名城”以及亚洲龙舟联合会总部所在地。

As a coastal place since ancient times, Foshan, where there are abundant swamps and water networks, has a long tradition of water god worship. The dragon is an important water god for Foshan people and its incarnation is the dragon boat. Dragon boating is to worship the dragon and pray for good weather and a bumper harvest. It has been a popular folk activity during the Dragon Boat Festival in every village of Foshan since the Ming and Qing dynasties. In the 21st century, dragon boating has developed in full swing and Foshan has become the "China Dragon Boat and Lion Dance Sports City" and the headquarters of the Asian Dragon Boat Federation.

顺德乐从龙舟队
Lecong Dragon Boat Team, Shunde

1.1 Origin of Foshan Dragon Boat Customs

Dragon boating is a time-honored, highly popular entertainment and sport around China. According to historical records, the Chinese characters of "dragon boat" first appeared in *Mu T'ien-tzu Chuan (The Chronicle of Mu, Son of Heaven)* that was allegedly written in the Warring States Period (475 B.C. - 221 B.C.), which says that the emperor travelled in a dragon-bird boat. In the later Warring States period, the famous patriotic poet Qu Yuan mentioned the dragon boat in his *Nine Songs*. The image of a dragon boat was found in the brocade painting "Man Taming the Dragon" which was unearthed from a Chu State tomb of the Warring States Period in Zidanku, Changsha, Hunan Province in 1973. In the center of the picture, a bearded man is rising to the Kingdom of Heaven on a giant dragon. The dragon holds its head and tail high while the body is flat. The whole thing is boat-shaped. This is the earliest dragon boat pattern found so far. From what is presented in the picture, this is a soul boat. The flying dragon is guiding the human soul to fly to the Kingdom of Heaven. It can thus be inferred that the dragon boat appeared no later than in the middle or late Warring States period.

Dragon boating appeared almost simultaneously with the dragon boat. A bronze battle-axe with the pattern of crest wearing men racing the dragon boat of the Spring and Autumn Period and the Warring States Period was unearthed in Shitu Mountain, Yinxian County (now Yinzhou District, Ningbo City), Zhejiang Province in 1976. This is a physical evidence of dragon boat racing. Dragon boat racing patterns are also found on a broken bronze drum unearthed in ancient tombs in Shizhai Mountain, Jinning District, Yunnan Province and on the upper surface of a bronze drum unearthed in an ancient tomb in Luobowan,

第一节 佛山龙舟习俗的起源

划龙舟是一项流传历史悠久、流行地区广阔、深受群众喜爱的民俗娱乐活动和体育运动。据文献考证，“龙舟”一词早在据传成书于战国时期的《穆天子传》中就出现了，“天子乘鸟舟龙卒浮于大沼”。晋郭璞注：“沼，池。龙下有舟字，舟皆以龙鸟为形制。”战国后期著名爱国诗人屈原所作《九歌》中有提到龙辀、水车，后世学者多认为就是指龙舟。1973年出土于湖南长沙子弹库战国楚墓的“人物御龙图”帛画中则有了龙舟的形象，画面中心绘一生须男子，驾驭着一条巨龙正向天国飞升。龙头、龙尾高昂，龙身平伏，整体呈舟形，此为迄今为止发现的最早的龙舟形图案。从画面呈现的意境看，此龙舟为魂舟，飞腾的龙引导人灵魂飞升天国。由此推断，龙舟最晚在战国中后期已经产生。

1973年出土于长沙子弹库战国楚墓的“人物御龙图”帛画（湖南省博物馆网站）
Brocade Painting “Man Taming the Dragon” Unearthed from a Chu State Tomb of the Warring States Period in Zidanku, Changsha, Hunan Province in 1973 (Website of Hunan Museum)

扒龙舟差不多与龙舟是同一时期出

古代越人的竞渡铜鼓图案（壮族在线）
Pattern of Dragon Boat Racing on a Bronze Drum of Ancient Yue Ethnic Group (www.Rauz.net)

现的。1976年浙江鄞县（今宁波市鄞州区）石秃山出土了春秋战国时期的羽人竞渡纹铜钺，上面刻有龙舟竞渡图案，龙舟竞渡终于有了实物佐证。此外，云南晋宁石寨山古墓群出土的一面残铜鼓和广西贵县罗泊湾汉墓出土的铜鼓上层，都有龙舟竞渡图像。深圳市南山博物馆藏的古越族青铜器中有战国靴形羽人船纹青铜钺、西汉变形羽人划船纹铜鼓，比石寨山类型稍晚。它们的时代相当于战国至东汉时间（公元前5世纪—公元1世纪），与龙舟产生的时代差不多。

记载龙舟竞渡的历史文献出现比较晚，据学者考证，最早记载龙舟竞渡的文献是三国时期吴国人周处所写的《风土记》，“仲夏端午，烹鹜、角黍……竞渡”。这说明三国两晋时期，龙舟竞渡已经成为江南地区的一种端午节俗。南北朝梁朝宗懔撰《荆楚岁时记》则提到了端午竞渡习俗的多种起源，还表明南北朝时期龙舟竞渡不止流行于吴地，还传播至荆楚、燕齐、吴越等地区。

到了唐代全盛时期，社会稳定，经济繁荣，节日娱乐民俗得到官府支持，龙舟竞渡尤为兴盛，不仅有如《隋唐嘉话》等历史文献

Guixian Country (now Guigang city), Guangxi Zhuang Autonomous Region. The boot-shaped bronze battle-axe with patterns of crest-wearing men in boats of the Warring States Period and the distorted bronze drum with patterns of crest-wearing men rowing boats of the Western Han Dynasty have a shorter history than that found in Shizhai Mountain. These artifacts of the ancient Yue nationality, stored in Shenzhen Nanshan Museum were from the Warring States Period to the Eastern Han Dynasty (5th century B.C. to 1st century A.D.), made in approximately the same period when the first dragon boat appeared.

Historical records of dragon boat racing appeared relatively late. According to scholars, the earliest one was found in *Feng Tu Ji (Records of Natural Conditions and Social Customs)* written by Zhou Chu from the State of Wu during the Three Kingdoms Period, which says that dragon boat races were held on the 5th day of the 5th lunar month in mid-summer. This indicates that during the Three Kingdoms Period and the Western and Eastern Jin dynasties, dragon boat racing was already a festive custom of the Double Fifth Festival in areas south of the Yangtze River. The various origins of the dragon boat racing are mentioned in *Jingchu Suishi Ji (Festivals and Customs in Jingchu Area)* written by Zong Lin of the State of Liang during the Northern and Southern Dynasties, indicating that such activities were popular not only in the State of Wu, but also in other regions such as Jingchu (Hubei Province), Yanqi (Hebei and Shandong provinces), and Wuyue (southern Jiangsu, Shanghai, Zhejiang, southern Anhui and northeast Jiangxi).

In the prime of the Tang Dynasty, which enjoyed social stability, economic prosperity, and official support for festive recreations and customs, dragon boat racing became especially popular. There were not only historical records in *Anecdotes of the Sui and Tang Dynasties*, but also large numbers of poems and songs describing the racing scenes, such as *Preface to Watching Dragon Boat Racing in Yangzhou* by the Tang Dynasty poet Luo Binwang and *The Song of Dragon Boat Racing* by Zhang Jianfeng which vividly describes the whole racing process. During the Tang Dynasty women were not prohibited from taking part in dragon boat racing. It was a vogue among the noble and celebrated classes to watch women's participation in dragon boat racing. For example, *Watching*

Dragon Boat Racing at Longtanxia, Guzhen by Li Zhen, the eighth son of Emperor Taizong of the Tang Dynasty, describes the scene of women's dragon boat racing at Xiashan, Guagndong Province.

Since the Song and Ming dynasties, there have been more abundant historical records of dragon boat racing, such as literati's notes, novels, and local chronicles. Dragon boat racing has become a popular folk entertainment all over China. According to *The Collection of Local Customs in China* compiled by Ding Shiliang and Zhao Fang, the custom of dragon boat racing spread widely in Hunan, Hubei, Guangdong, Guangxi, Fujian, Zhejiang, Jiangsu, Anhui, Jiangxi, Sichuan, Yunnan, Guizhou, Hong Kong, Macao and Taiwan, which are mainly located in the southeast, southwest, central China and coastal regions. There were also dragon boat races in some other places where there was a water shortage, such as Xi'an in Shaanxi, Kaifeng in Henan, and Beijing. Since the Tang Dynasty, records of emperors watching dragon boat races at the waterfront show that such activities were also popular in the northern regions. In Volume 21 of *Gai Yu Cong Kao* (Reading Notes While Taking Care of My Parents) by Zhao Yi of the Ming Dynasty, Emperor Jingzong and Emperor Muzong of the Ming Dynasty respectively watched the dragon boat racing at the Aquatic Palace. In *Life in the Eastern Capital* by Meng Yuanlao of the Song Dynasty, the emperors and court officials of the Song Dynasty held banquets by the Riverside Hall of Jinming Pool, where there were performances by colored boats, small boats, music boats, painting boats, small dragon boats, tiger head boats, flying fish boats, loach boats and large dragon boats. Emperors of the Ming Dynasty watched dragon boats at Ziguangge of Zhongnanhai. In the Qing Dynasty, Emperor Qianlong and Emperor Jiaqing once watched dragon boat racing at Fuhai Lake of Yuanmingyuan Park. Now, dragon boat racing, a popular folk entertainment and sport in China, has become an important means for the governments to enhance the local image and boost cultural and economic development.

There are different assumptions about the origins of dragon boat racing. Among them, the most widely spread ones include commemoration of heroes, worship of the dragon totem, avoidance of evil spirits, and sacrifice to water gods.

记载，还出现了大量描述龙舟竞渡场景的诗词歌赋。例如：著名诗人骆宾王的《扬州看竞渡序》，对龙舟竞渡进行了生动描述；张建封的《竞渡歌》则将整个竞渡过程描述得惟妙惟肖。唐代时期龙舟竞渡还没有女性禁忌，观看女性参加的龙舟竞渡是达官贵人都热衷的风雅之事，如唐太宗第八子越王李贞在《鼓镇龙潭峡观竞渡》中描写了其在广东峡山观竞渡时女龙竞渡的情景。

宋明以来，关于扒龙舟的各种资料更为丰富，文人笔记、小说、各地地方史志等都有大量记载，大江南北扒龙舟风俗盛行，扒龙舟已经成为一种普遍性的娱乐民俗活动。据丁世良、赵放主编的《中国地方志民俗资料汇编》，扒龙舟的风俗广泛分布于湖南、湖北、广东、广西、福建、浙江、江苏、安徽、江西、四川、云南、贵州、香港、澳门、台湾等地，主要集中于中国的东南、西南、中部和沿海大部分地区。甚至在缺水的中国北方如陕西西安、河南开封、北京某些地方也有龙舟竞渡。自唐以降，各朝皇帝临水观竞渡的记载充分表明了龙舟竞渡在北方地区也受欢迎。赵翼的《陔余丛考》卷二十一载：“（敬宗）幸鱼藻宫观竞渡。……（穆宗）九月观竞渡于鱼藻宫……”宋孟元老《东京梦华录》亦记宋朝君臣在金明池临水殿集宴，有彩舟、小船、乐船、画船、小龙船、虎头船、飞鱼船、鳅鱼船、大龙船等表演。明代皇帝在中南海紫光阁观龙舟，清代则在圆明园的福海举行竞渡，乾隆、嘉庆等均曾前往观看。到了现代，龙舟竞渡发展得如火如荼，已经成为大江南北各地人们喜爱的民俗娱乐活动和体育运动，也成了政府提升当地形象、推动文化和经济发展的重要手段之一。

龙舟竞渡历史悠久，流传地区广泛，文化底蕴深厚，关于龙舟竞渡的起源众说纷纭。龙舟竞渡起源诸说中流传最为广泛的主要为纪念英雄人物说、龙图腾祭说、辟邪禳灾说、祭祀水神说。此外，还有探亲访友说、锻炼水中技能说、夏至“飞龙在天”的天象说、祭“地腊”说，这几种影响较小。

龙舟竞渡起源众说纷纭，且大都能自圆其说，各有各的道理。龙舟竞渡流传地域广泛，大江南北均有龙舟竞渡的习俗，但它们的起源不一定是同一的，还必须联系当地独特的自然人文环境，才能正确解释当地龙舟竞渡的起源。笔者认为，佛山乃至整个广府地区的龙舟竞渡都是源于水神崇拜。

佛山位于珠江三角洲腹地。距今五六千年前，还是典型的海洋地貌，有很多被大海环绕的岛屿，后来三角洲陆地不断扩展，有了成片的平原。佛山境内水道纵横，河湖密布，同时因其地处亚热带，气候温和，雨量充沛，形成了多水多雨的特殊地理环境和气候。佛山多水多雨的特殊地理环境和气候，既给佛山人带来了便利，也带来了频繁的洪涝灾害。在科学还不发达的古代社会，人们未能对这些自然物和自然现象形成正确的认识，他们认为水是一种神奇的东西，在水的背后肯定存在一种不可捉摸的、神秘的主宰力

老龙头
Old Dragon Head

In addition, there are also some less influential ones like visiting friends and relatives, training water skills, celebrating the celestial phenomenon of "the flying dragon in the sky" at the Summer Solstice and sacrificing to *Dila* (namely, the Double Fifth Festival of the lunar calendar).

Most of these assumptions about the origins of dragon boat racing are justifiable. However, because of the widespread popularity of dragon boat racing in all parts of China, the origins are not necessarily the same. It is advisable to take the unique natural and humanistic environment into consideration. It is believed that dragon boat racing in Foshan and even the whole Cantonese region has originated from water god worship.

Foshan is located in the center of the Pearl River Delta. About five or six thousand years ago, it still had a typical marine landform with many islands surrounded by the sea. Later because of the constant expansion of the Pearl River Delta, a plain with a crisscross water network has been formed. With mild subtropical climate and abundant rainfall, the city enjoys special geographical environment and climate, which bring the Foshan people both convenience and frequent floods. In ancient times when science was not developed, people failed to have a correct understanding of these natural things and phenomena. Instead, they thought that water was magic, behind which was surely some intangible yet mysterious dominating force, hence, the water god worship, a product of agricultural civilization. Such worship is flourishing in Foshan, where there are various water gods, including Nanhai Zhaoming Dragon King, the Dragon Mother, King Zhenwu, Mazu, and the turtle god, among whom the dragon god is most important.

The dragon is an imaginary being by the Chinese people and one of the four divine beasts symbolizing auspice in the Chinese culture, namely, the dragon, the phoenix, the kylin and the turtle. The dragon is regarded as a symbol of prosperity and authorization by heaven. Moreover, it is a water god. For example, people pray to the earth dragon and the responsive dragon for rain. Oracles for praying to the earth dragon for rain show that as early as in the Shang and Zhou dynasties, the dragon was already regarded as the master of rain or the water god. *Shan Hai Jing (The Classic of Mountains and Seas)* and other ancient writings have similar descriptions while archaeological findings provide direct evidence. For example, on the bottom of a colored pottery basin which is 4,500 years from now unearthed at the site of Taosi, Xiangfen, Shanxi Province is painted a coiled dragon with a crocodile head and a snake body, and a paddy rice seedling in its mouth. The custom of praying to the dragon and associating it with the harvest of paddy rice conveys people's wish for favorable weather and abundant grains.

In *Chunqiu Fanlu (The Luxuriant Dew of the Spring and Autumn)*, a philosophical-mythological work centered on the induction of heaven and men by Dong Zhongshu of the Han Dynasty, there are meticulous descriptions of praying to the earth dragon for rain, including the changing colors of the dragon in accordance with the seasons, the color of the dancers' dresses being the same as that of the dragon. In drought periods of the Sui Dynasty, the emperors had earth dragons made to pray for rain. In the Tang Dynasty, with large numbers of Buddhist classics introduced into China, Buddhist culture was at its prime. Naga (meaning "snake") in Indian Buddhism shares something in common with the Chinese dragon in that both of them have the function of administering rain and water. Influenced by Buddhism, the Chinese dragon has its functions enhanced to control the clouds and administer rain, thus becoming the most important water god in China.

Since the Tang Dynasty, the increasingly higher status of the dragon king as a rain master has resulted in the merging of the two images. Therefore, people prayed specially to the dragon king for rain and emperors endowed and offered sacrifices to the dragon kings. For example, in 751 A.D. , Emperor Xuanzong of the Tang Dynasty endowed the East Sea with the title of King of the Grand Virtue, the South Sea with the King of Grand Benefits, the West Sea with the King of Grand Moisture and the North Sea with the King of Grand Luster. The Song Dynasty carried on the practice of worshiping the five dragons in the east, west, north, south, and the central area. In October 1108, Emperor Huizong of the Song Dynasty named the dragons of five directions kings. Later, boosted by folk beliefs and witchcraft, the status of the dragon as a water god was further strengthened. Where there is water, there is the dragon king, who is responsible for preventing flood, drought and poor harvest.

量，最终形成了水神崇拜。水神崇拜是自然崇拜的一种，它是农业文明发展的产物。佛山的水神崇拜十分兴盛，水神五花八门，有南海昭明龙王、龙母、真武帝君、妈祖、龟神等，龙神是佛山十分重要的水神。

龙是中国人想象出来的神物，是中国文化象征祥瑞的四灵兽——龙、凤、麒麟、龟之一，龙的出现被看作盛世或受天命的象征。龙更被视为司水之神，传说中的土龙、应龙都是祈雨的对象。甲骨卜有作土龙求雨的卜辞，这说明早在商周时代，龙就已经被人们视作雨师或司水之神。《山海经·大荒东经》中有应龙降雨说，敦煌所出写本《瑞应图》“青龙”一章也是将龙视为司水之神。考古资料则提供了更为直观的证据，例如山西襄汾陶寺遗址出土的距今4500年的彩陶盆，底部的彩绘蟠龙鳄首蛇身，口里衔着一根禾苗。将稻谷丰收与龙联系起来的祷龙习俗是希望风调雨顺，五谷丰登。

汉代董仲舒的《春秋繁露》是一部以天人感应为核心的哲学—神学著作，其中关于作土龙求雨的内容描述得非常细致，如龙的颜色随季节的变化而变化，祈雨舞者的衣服颜色与龙的颜色必须一致，等等。隋旱时，“令人家造土龙。雨澍，则命有司报”。唐时，佛教文化极度繁荣，大量印度佛教经典传入中原。印度佛教中的那伽（梵语NAGA，意为“蛇”）因为与中国的龙有共同之处，遂被汉译为“龙”。那伽之所以被古代印度人民崇拜，主要与它司水布雨的职能有关。由于受到佛教的影响，中国龙的行云布雨功能得到加强，使得龙成了中国最重要的水神。

唐代以降，龙王作为雨师的地位愈来愈高，最终使得龙王与雨师形象重合，人们遂专门向龙王祈雨，皇帝也郑重其事地对龙王加封、祭祀。唐天宝十年（751）正月二十三日，唐玄宗“封东海为广德王，南海为广利王，西海为广润王，北海为广泽王”。宋代沿用唐代祭五龙之制，大观二年（1108）十月，宋徽宗赵佶将五方龙封王。后来在民间信仰和巫术的推动下，龙作为司水之神的地位进一步巩固，凡有水之处就驻有龙王，专门负责当地水旱歉收的问题。

屈大均的《广东新语》有广东人向龙神求雨的记载。在佛山民间，龙就是司水之神，是江河的主管，地方史志对此多有记载。民国《佛山忠义乡志》卷八《祠祀》龙母庙条目云：“龙能致云雨泽万物，国朝已有祀典，故龙母庙载入庙宇类。”民国《顺德县志》载，龙江的龙穴山据说为龙穴，能出云降雨。南海九江沙嘴村的龙王宫碑文，再现了九江人对水神龙的虔诚信仰。

南海九江沙嘴村龙王宫碑文
Inscription in the Dragon King Palace in Shazui Village, Jiujiang, Nanhai

因为视龙为司水之神，佛山一直流传着舞龙求雨的习俗。在佛山，四月初八是民间舞飞龙求雨的节日，“飞龙”就是三节木龙。因舞龙不在水上，而在陆地举行，人们习惯称“飞龙”为

In *Guangdong Xinyu (New Notes on Guangdong)* written by Qu Dajun, there are descriptions of the Guangdong people praying to the dragon for rain. Various local chronicles also indicate that the dragon is the water god and the administrator of rivers to the Foshan people. For example, the entry Dragon Mother Temple in *Temple Worship*, Vol. 8 of *Chronicle of Foshan, Town of Loyalty and Righteousness* says, "The dragon can create clouds and rain to moisten everything. The imperial court has sacrificial rituals, so the Dragon Mother Temple falls into the category of temples." According to *Shunde County Chronicle*, Longxue (Dragon Lair) Mountain in Longjiang is believed to be the dragon lair and is capable of producing clouds and rain. The inscription in the Dragon King Palace in Shazui Village, Jiujiang, Nanhai represents the pious belief of the Jiujiang people in the dragon, the water god.

南海九江沙嘴村龙王宫
Dragon King Palace in Shazui Village, Jiujiang, Nanhai

As the dragon is regarded as the water god, the custom of dragon dancing to pray for rain has had a long history in Foshan. In this city, the eighth day of the fourth lunar month is the festival of dancing the flying dragon for rain. The flying dragon is a three-section wooden one. As the dragon dance takes place on land, the dragon is customarily called "dry dragon", hence the name "dancing the dry dragon". In the Qing Dynasty, the custom of dancing the flying dragon was popular in Shaluopu, Chancheng, Foshan. On that day, three strong men, respectively holding the dragon head, body and tail, which were carved out of choice mahogany, performed the tumbling and flying of the dragon with the southern school martial arts. At that time, flying the dry dragon not only meant to pray for rain, but also for blessings and for avoidance of disasters, rendering the occasion festive. The Foshan folk song "Dancing Dragon for Rain" vividly describes Foshan people's good wishes. As the dragon is the water god, people have to offer sacrifices to the dragon god if they want fine weather and bumper harvests. One of the rituals in Foshan is the dragon boat racing. A substantial evidence of Foshan people's water worship of dragon boats is the tablet with the words meaning "spreading water and generating life", presented by the Yanbu villagers to their Pantang counterparts in the Old Dragon Ritual of Yanbu, Nanhai, Foshan. As Pantang is crisscrossed by water, its crops rely heavily on rainwater and climate. Every year, when the Yanbu Old Dragon pays a visit, the locals have to open the flood gate to bring in water, which moistens their crops and leads to a bumper harvest. Therefore, the Pantang and Yanbu people all believe that the Old Dragon boat has the magic power of "spreading water and generating life".

Foshan dragon boat racing does not necessarily take place during the Dragon Boat Festival, but mainly in the fourth and fifth lunar months. *Guangdong Tongzhi (General Records of Guangdong)* written by Huang Zuo during the Jiajing period of the Qing Dynasty meticulously lists the customs of dragon boat racing in prefectures of Shaozhou, Huizhou, Chaozhou, Zhaoqing, Leizhou, and Qiongzhou. *Nanhai County Chronicle* written during the Kangxi period of the Qing Dynasty vividly describes the boisterous and magnificent scenes of dragon boat racing.

Dragon boat racing in Guangdong is not only held during the Dragon Boat Festival, but also on other dates. The poem "Yuan Xi"(The Lantern Festival) by Wen Tianxiang of the Southern Song Dynasty, describes the unprecedented scene of dragon boat racing in Nanhai County on the night of the Lantern Festival.

Some villages in Sanshui, Foshan choose to race dragon boats during some folk festivals. For example, Zhushan Village, Leping Town sets it on the third day

黄岐龙母庙
Huangqi Dragon Mother Temple

“旱龙”，故有“舞旱龙”之名。清代时，舞飞龙之俗在佛山禅城沙洛铺一带流行，当天居民用上好红木雕刻成龙头、龙身、龙尾各一段，由三个精壮男子各举一段，运用南派武技表演龙腾翻滚飞舞的技艺。当时佛山舞飞龙既有求雨的目的，也有祈福避灾、营造节日气氛的成分。佛山民谣《舞龙求雨歌》以活泼的语言将佛山人舞龙求雨的美好心愿生动地刻画了出来。

龙为司水之神，要想风调雨顺、五谷丰登、蚕丰鱼肥，就得祭祀龙神。而龙舟就是龙的化身，在佛山祭祀龙神的仪式之一就是龙舟竞渡，这就是佛山龙舟竞渡的源起。佛山南海盐步老龙礼俗活动中，盐步乡亲曾送给了泮塘乡亲一块“播液发灵”牌匾，正是佛山人对龙舟水信仰的明证。由于泮塘地处水网地带，农作物受雨水气候的影响极大。每年盐步老龙到访，当地人为迎接老龙需开闸引水，这些水浇灌、滋润农作物后，农作物均获得丰收，因而泮塘人和盐步人均相信老龙龙船水有“播液发灵”的奇效。

佛山龙舟竞渡的日期并不一定都在端午节，主要集中在农历四、五两个月。明嘉靖黄佐纂的《广东通志》详细列出韶州府、惠州府、潮州府、肇庆府、雷州府、琼州府等地的端午龙舟竞渡习俗。清康熙《南海县志》对端午龙舟竞渡的场面描述得很生动，热闹非凡、景象壮观的游龙场面仿若画轴在眼前展开。

广府地域的龙舟竞渡除了作为端午节俗外，也会在其他日子举行。南宋文天祥的《元夕》诗，描述了当时南海县正月十五龙舟竞渡的情景：“南海观元夕，兹游古未曾。人间大竞渡，水上小烧灯。”

佛山三水的一些村落会选择在民俗节日期间进行比赛：乐平

镇竹山村在农历三月初三赛龙舟，寓意龙抬头、事业蒸蒸日上；五顶岗上官员村的村民都拜龙母，在农历五月初八龙母诞举办龙舟比赛，祈求风调雨顺；潮州府则是在四月初一划龙舟，“潮阳四月朔日，粗磨农村金鼓喧阗，谓之‘转龙船’”。

屈大均《广东新语》之“广州时序”载广州四月初八开始扒龙舟：“四月八日浴佛，采面荭榔，捣百花叶为饼，是日江上陈龙舟，曰出水龙，潮田始作。”是日之后，龙船金鼓咚锵声响远近可闻。

广宁、新宁、归善、揭阳、鹤山、博罗、化州等地则在农历五月初一开始龙舟竞渡，五六日乃止。南海九江人竞渡从五月初开始，一直延续到寒秋九月。

为什么广东龙舟竞渡主要在四、五月举行呢？在农耕社会，四、五两个月是广东极为重要的时候，尤其是五月，此时正是早稻抽穗扬花、果树开花结果时，风调雨顺的气候就非常重要。但广东的四、五月是天气最多变的时期，台风、暴雨奄忽而至，若大水冲决堤坝、淹没田园，最后将导致人们颗粒无收。古人认为这些风暴都是由龙神带来的，必须祭祀龙神，取悦它们，才能求得风调雨顺，因此要举行龙舟竞渡。

of the third lunar month, meaning that when the dragon looks up, businesses will be thriving. In Shangguanyuan Village, Wudinggang Town, all the villagers worship the Dragon Mother, so they hold dragon boat racing on her birthday, the eighth day of the fifth lunar month to pray for good weather. In Chaozhou Prefecture, dragon boats are rowed on the first day of the fourth lunar month.

"Dates of Canton" in *New Notes on Guangdong* by Qu Dajun records that dragon boating starts on the eighth day of the fourth lunar month in Guangzhou, "On the eighth day of the fourth lunar month, the Buddha is bathed. Pancakes are made from yams and leaves of various plants. The dragon boats are lifted out of water. This is the time to start the spring planting." From this day on, the drumbeats from the dragon boats can be heard far and near.

In places such as Guangning, Xinning, Guishan, Jieyang, Heshan, Boluo and Huazhou, dragon boat racing starts from the first day of the fifth lunar month and lasts for five or six days. In Jiujiang, Nanhai, it starts from the beginning of the fifth lunar month and lasts until the ninth in autumn.

Dragon boat racing in Guangdong takes place mainly in the fourth and fifth lunar months because in agricultural society, these two months are extremely important in this province. In the fifth lunar month, early paddy rice ears and trees blossom and bear fruits, so good weather is vital. But in these two months, the weather is most changeable, with frequent and unpredictable typhoons and storms breaking dams and submerging fields, leaving people nothing for harvest. The ancient people believed that all these were brought by the dragon gods so they had to worship and please them for good weather, hence the dragon boat racing.

1.2 The Development of Dragon Boat Racing in Foshan

Before the Tang and Song dynasties, Lingnan, surrounded by oceans and sporadic deltas and islands, had few residents, most of whom made their living on boat. Qu Dajun once said: "Guangdong is a land of water where most people make their living on boat." and "Cantonese are good at using boats". Thus, Guangdong enjoys a long history of boat. However, it is impossible to tell when dragon boat racing started in Guangdong. On the upper side of The bronze drum unearthed from an ancient tomb in Luobowan, Guixian Country (now Guigang city), Cuangxi Zhuang Autonomous Region, the Baiye bronze battle-axe and drum collected in Shenzhen Nanshan Museum, and the murals in Zuojiang Valley in Guangxi Zhuang Autonomous Region also show vivid scenes of dragon boat racing. All have patterns of, which means that dragon boat racing began to emerge in Lingnan no later than the Eastern Han Dynasty.

As early as in the Tang Dynasty, Guangdong saw large-scale dragon boat races. Li Zhen's poem mentioned above not only vividly describes the scale and intensity of dragon boat races back then, but also women's elegant demeanor in the races. Another legend has it that the Southern Han governor Liu Gong who had the Yuye Pool (now near Yaozhou Site, Xihu Road) dredged in west Guangzhou, held dragon boat races every year during the Dragon Boat Festival which were participated by women as well. Both records mention women's participation in dragon boat racing, indicating that women were not prohibited from dragon boat racing at that time, in sharp contrast to later practices.

In the Song Dynasty, dragon boating flourished for a long time. Races were not only held during the Dragon Boat Festival but also during the Lantern Festival on the 15th day on the first lunar month. "The Things I saw during the Dragon

第二节　佛山龙舟竞渡的发展历程

唐宋以前，岭南被大海环绕，偶有一些岛屿，鲜少居人，居民大都以舟楫为生，屈大钧曾云“广为水国，人多以舟楫为食”“越人善用舟”“越人善操舟”，因此广府地区用舟的历史非常悠久。然而，广府龙舟竞渡究竟起于何时，已不可考。广西贵县罗泊湾铜鼓，深圳市南山博物馆收藏的百越青铜钺、铜鼓，广西左江流域的崖壁画，都有龙舟竞渡图案，说明至迟在东汉，岭南地区已经有了龙舟竞渡习俗。

古代越人的竞渡铜鼓图案（壮族在线）
Pattern of Dragon Boat Racing on a Bronze Drum of Ancient Yue Ethnic Group (www.Rauz.net)

唐时广东已经有了大规模的龙舟竞渡，《全唐诗》中李贞的《鼓镇龙潭峡观竞渡》描写诗人在广东峡山观竞渡的情形。诗人不仅描述了当时竞渡的规模和激烈程度，还用神来之笔点出了女性竞渡的风采。又传说南汉后主刘龚当年在广州城西疏浚“玉液池”（现广州市西湖路药洲遗址附近），每年农历端午节举行龙舟竞渡，且有女性参与。两处均提到了女性参与龙舟竞渡，说明当时龙舟活动还没有禁止女性参与，这与后来龙舟活动禁止女性参与大相径庭。

南海九江女子龙舟队
Women’s Dragon Boat Team of Jiujiang, Nanhai

宋代时期扒龙舟活动长盛不衰，其竞渡时间不只在端午节，正月十五也有龙舟竞渡。北宋曲江人余靖的《端午日事》诗云：“江上何人吊屈原，但闻风俗彩舟轻。空斋无事同儿戏，学系朱丝辟五兵。”前文提及的南宋文天祥的《元夕》诗，就描述了当时南海县正月十五进行龙舟竞渡的情景。

明清至民国时期，广东各州各县龙舟活动已经非常普遍，广东地方史志中有大量记载，如《广东通志》《广东府志》《南海县

Boat Festival", a poem by Yu Jing from Qujiang (now in Shaoguan, Guangdong) in the Northern Song Dynasty describes dragon boating during the Dragon Boat Festival while "The Lantern Festival" by Wen Tianxiang mentioned above describes dragon boat racing in Nanhai County during the Lantern Festival.

From the Ming and Qing dynasties to the Republic of China period, there were widespread dragon boat races in Guangdong, as evidenced by a large number of records in local chronicles such as *General Records of Guangdong, Guangdong Prefectural Chronicle, Nanhai County Chronicle* and township chronicles.

In the Ming and Qing dynasties, dragon boat racing became a popular folk entertainment in Foshan. The Yanbu Old Dragon boat custom in Nanhai has been handed down for a few hundred years, demonstrating the popularity of dragon boat racing in Guangzhou and Foshan and the close ties between the two cities in dragon boat culture. During the Wanli period of the Ming Dynasty, the Yanbu and the Pantang dragon boats became "father and adopted son" by chance. From then on, the Yanbu Old Dragon visits his "adopted son" in Liwan, Guangzhou in the fifth lunar month every year. The Yanbu Old Dragon is believed to be the oldest existing dragon boat in China, dating back to 1432, i.e. more than 580 years ago.

Shunde County Chronicle during the Wanli period of the Ming Dynasty also mentions, "Every village makes its own dragon boat to welcome the dragon god for a tour amid drumbeats." The fabulous and exciting dragon boat racing attracted people of different social ranks to participate. According to the *Chronicle*, Liang Yuanzhu, a successful candidate in the highest imperial examinations from Shunde, once watched dragon boat racing in 1622.

In the Qing Dynasty, the traditional dragon boat activities in Foshan were still very popular. Both versions of *Nanhai County Chronicle* during the Kangxi period (1622-1722) and the Qianlong period (1736-1795) describe dragon boat racing during the Dragon Boat Festival: officials and common folks gathered lotuses and watched dragon boat racing for five days. *Nanhai County Chronicle* during the Daoguang period (1821-1850) further emphasizes the customs of dragon boat racing during the Dragon Boat Festival in Nanhai County and specifically mentions the Dragon Boat Gala in Huangzhuqi Village (now

Huangqi in Nanhai, Foshan).

In the Qing Dynasty, the tradition of dragon boat racing was also prevalent in Shunde, about which both versions of *Nanhai County Chronicle* during the Kangxi and Qianlong periods describe like this: "During the Dragon Boat Festival, people make Zongzi and drink wine from Changyang; they attach tigers made of folium artemisiae argyi above their gates. Besides, every village makes its own dragon boat to welcome the dragon god for a tour amid drumbeats." The stone plaque that reads "Defeating Other Dragons" earned by the winner of the dragon boat race in 1699 is still preserved in Beishui Village, Xingtan Town, Shunde. It is an evidence of the booming dragon boat races in Shunde at that time.

Longshan was one of the places in Shunde where dragon boat races enjoyed the most popularity. In 1784, Wen Rushi, a successful candidate in the highest imperial examinations, wrote a poem describing the intensity of the dragon boat races and the binge-drinking celebrations after the win. In the early Qing Dynasty, Qu Dajun recorded in his *New Notes on Guangdong* the time, waterway requirements, and rules of dragon boat races in Longjiang, Shunde. His records enable readers to have a comprehensive understanding of dragon boat racing and

2018年6月16日龙眼村游龙

Dragon Boat Cruise of Longyan Village on June 16th, 2018

志》及各地乡志均有关于扒龙舟的详细记载。

明清时期，龙舟竞渡已经成为佛山各地风行的一种民俗娱乐活动。南海盐步流传了几百年的盐步老龙礼俗，展示了明时广佛一带龙舟竞渡的兴盛和两地龙舟文化的紧密联系。明万历年间，盐步与泮塘的龙舟因缘结契，此后盐步老龙每年五月会去广州荔湾探望“契仔”泮塘龙舟，这艘老龙船据说是目前中国最古老的龙舟，其历史可追溯到明宣德七年（1432），至今已有580多年。

明万历《顺德县志》亦云：“乡村为龙舟，迎神出游，鼓吹杂还。”精彩激烈的龙舟活动，吸引了士庶各色人等参与。《顺德县志》载，明天启二年（1622），顺德进士梁元柱“尝观竞渡”。

清代佛山传统龙舟活动依然盛极一时。清康熙、乾隆版《南海县志》都描述了南海县端午节的龙舟竞渡：“士庶采莲观竞渡，五日乃至。”道光《南海县志》进一步强调了南海县端午节龙舟竞渡的习俗，并特别提到了黄竹岐堡（今佛山南海区黄岐）的锦龙盛会。

清代顺德龙舟竞渡习俗氛围也非常浓厚。清康熙、乾隆版《顺德县志》均有龙舟竞渡习俗描述：“端午酿角黍，饮昌阳酒，缚艾虎于门，乡村为龙舟，迎神出游，鼓吹杂还。”至今保留在顺德杏坛镇北水村的一块清康熙己卯年（1699）龙舟竞渡第一名所得“力压群龙”石牌匾，是反映当年顺德龙舟竞渡盛况的重要实物。

龙山是当时顺德龙舟竞渡最为兴盛的地方之一。清乾隆四十九年（1784），进士温汝适就写了一首《龙山竹枝词》：“飞棹凌波擂鼓催，龙舟迟疾去还来。炊成赤稻千夫饭，赢得津头斗酒回。”描写了龙山龙舟竞渡的龙船鼓、竞渡、龙船饭、标部等，再现了当时龙舟夺标的紧张激烈和夺标得胜后的豪饮庆祝场面。清初屈大均在其笔记体著作《广东新语》中详细记载了顺德龙江龙舟竞渡的时间、水道要求、规则。屈大均的记载让读者对龙江龙舟竞渡有了全面的了解，从中也可看出龙舟竞渡在顺德龙江盛行的原因。

高明古孟村龙舟
Dragon Boat of Gu’meng Village, Gaoming

三水和高明地处西北江三角洲上游，河涌水网相较于下游的南海、顺德较少，但其地龙舟竞渡习俗依然风行。清康熙、嘉庆版《三水县志》记载的端午节俗中均有龙舟竞渡，竞渡得胜称为夺锦，还要簪花挂红。清康熙、道光、光绪版《高明县志》同样记载了高明县（今佛山市高明区）的龙舟竞渡习俗：“端午：饮菖蒲艾酒，食角黍，观龙舟竞渡。”

the reasons for its popularity in Longjiang.

Sanshui and Gaoming are located in the upper reaches of the Delta of the Xijiang and Beijiang rivers, where there are fewer water networks than in Nanhai and Shunde in the lower reaches, but the custom of dragon boat racing there is equally popular. Both versions of *Sanshui County Chronicle* during the Kangxi period and the Jiaqing period (1796-1820) record dragon boat racing during the Dragon Boat Festival, the winner boat of which would be decorated with flowers and red silk. The three versions of *Gaoming County Chronicle* during the Kangxi period, the Daoguang period and the Guangxu period(1871-1908) also mention

the custom of dragon boat racing in Gaoming County (now Gaoming District, Foshan): "Dragon Boat Festival: Drink calamus and absinthe wine, eat Zongzi and watch dragon boat racing".

In the Ming and Qing dynasties, Foshan (now Chancheng District, Foshan) also had the tradition of watching dragon boat racing during the Dragon Boat Festival, but with fewer people familiar with water skills. The craze for dragon boat racing wore off, and boats were used mainly for travelling.

During the period of the Republic of China (1912-1949), dragon boat racing that had been popular for hundreds of years saw a slight decline due to wars and other reasons. After the founding of the People's Republic of China in 1949, the traditional dragon boat custom experienced a short recovery. However, due to economic difficulties, dragon boat races were only held once several years, especially when there were major celebrations. During the "Cultural Revolution" (1966-1976), dragon boat activities were forbidden.

Since the end of the "Cultural Revolution", the custom of dragon boat racing in Foshan has gradually resumed thanks to supportive policies. The Foshan people lifted the survived old dragon boats buried deep in the rivers and had them repaired. In villages which had no old dragon boats left, the villagers and their overseas compatriots were all eager to donate money to make new ones.

Since the mid-1980s, dragon boats in Foshan have developed in two prongs. On the one hand, professional dragon boat teams have entered a golden development period with the evolving professionalization. On the other hand, villages and towns were also keen on holding dragon boat activities, which have attracted hundreds of thousands of people every year and served as a grand event during the Dragon Boat Festival, the National Day and other festivals.

In 1984, Jiujiang Dragon Boat Team was officially established. During the Dragon Boat Festival in the following year, it won the championship in the Macao International Dragon Boat Races. The team then claimed the championship in the following three consecutive years. The honors have earned the team great fame. Since the 1990s, Jiujiang Dragon Boat Team, by cooperating with enterprises, has become professionalized and developed rapidly. Since it won the championship in the 1999 Hong Kong International Dragon Boat Races, it claimed the title for six more years on end until 2006. In 2010, Jiujiang Men's Dragon Boat Team beat China's National Dragon Boat Team, thus being entitled to compete in the Asian Games on behalf of China. Since 2011, Jiujiang Women's Dragon Boat Team has become a frequent champion in China Longzhou Tournament. Shunde Men's Dragon Boat Team and Shunde Women's Dragon Boat Team were established in 1983 and 1985 respectively. As of the end of 1990, Shunde Men's Team had won the first place in the first four races and the second place in the fifth one in five "Qu Yuan Cup" Dragon Boat

明清时期的佛山（今佛山禅城区）也有端午节观龙舟竞渡的习俗，但熟悉水性者日少，故竞渡之风不炽，居民大都是乘舫出游。

进入民国之后，因受到战乱等原因的影响，佛山风行了数百年的竞渡之风稍颓。中华人民共和国成立后，传统龙舟习俗有一个短暂的恢复期，但由于经济比较困难，都是间隔几年才举行一次龙舟赛，大都是选择有重大庆典活动的时候举办。“文化大革命”开始，龙舟活动被禁止。

“文化大革命”结束后，佛山龙舟竞渡习俗乘着政策的春风逐渐恢复。佛山民众非常兴奋，纷纷将深埋在河涌中的幸存老龙舟起出来修理。没有幸存老龙舟的村落，群众积极捐资制造新龙舟，海外乡亲也纷纷解囊相助。

20世纪80年代以来，佛山龙舟的发展是“一花两叶”。随着职业化发展的推进，佛山龙舟专业队伍进入了发展的黄金时期，同时乡镇村落也热衷于举办龙舟活动，每年都会吸引数十万民众参与，成为端午、国庆等节日期间的盛事。

1984年，九江龙舟队正式成立。翌年端午，九江龙舟队首次跻身澳门国际龙舟邀请赛，最终夺得冠军，并在此后的3年中蝉联冠军，夺下四连冠，九江龙舟名号因此响彻四方。20世纪90年代后，九江龙舟队与企业联合，步入职业化道路，获得了大发展，并于1999年获得香港国际龙舟邀请赛冠军，至2006年，实现了此赛事的七连冠。2010年，九江男子龙舟队发挥出色，战胜了国家集训队，获得了为国出征亚运会的资格。2011年以来，九江女子龙舟队成为中华龙舟大赛常胜将军，数次夺得冠军头衔。顺德男、女龙舟队分

2013 年10月1日九江传统龙舟赛现场
Scene of Jiujiang Traditional Dragon Boat Racing on Oct. 1st, 2013

别组建于1983年和1985年。至1990年底，在5届全国“屈原杯”龙舟赛中，男队获第一至四届冠军和第五届亚军。2013年9月，顺德龙舟俱乐部乐从龙舟队代表国家前往韩国参加第十届亚洲龙舟锦标赛，夺得3金3银；10月，该队再次披上战袍，代表中国征战东亚运动会，斩获2金1银1铜。顺德乐从龙舟队男队有“准国家队”的称号，在2011年以来的中华龙舟大赛中屡获佳绩，在2016、2017年度总成绩排行榜上排名第一。

近年来，佛山各地龙舟文化蓬勃发展，每年端午、国庆等节日前后，威武雄壮的龙舟在河涌间穿梭往来，龙船锣鼓咚咚作响，龙船饭飘出诱人的香味，噼啪的鞭炮声此起彼伏，宁静的水乡沸腾了。佛山扒龙舟活动中，最激动人心的环节要数龙舟竞渡。近年来

Races. In September 2013, Lecong Dragon Boat Team from Shunde Dragon Boat Club, on behalf of China, participated in the 10th Asian Dragon Boat Championships held in Korea, securing 3 gold and 3 silver. In October that year, the team, on behalf of China again, won 2 gold, 1 silver and 1 bronze in the East Asian Games. Shunde Lecong Men's Team, which is called the "Quasi National Team", has performed impressively since 2011, ranking the first in terms of total scores in 2016 and 2017.

In recent years, dragon-boat-related cultures have prospered in Foshan. Every year around such festivals as the Dragon Boat Festival and the National Day, grand and powerful dragon boats shuttle in creeks, amid the beats of drums and gongs. There was also the inviting smell of the dragon boat meals and the

"扒龙舟"瓷盘描绘的珠江彩龙竞艳（趁景），高6.9厘米、口径41.2厘米、底径21.5厘米（佛山市博物馆）

Pearl River Colored Dragon Boat Pageant Depicted in "Dragon Boating" on a Porcelain Plate with a Height of 6.9 cm, an Upper Diameter of 41.2 cm and a Bottom Diameter of 21.5 cm (Foshan Museum)

continuous crackling firecrackers. Among the dragon boat activities in Foshan, the most exciting one is dragon boat racing. Villages and towns have been keen on holding dragon boat activities of different scales, including races within the village, among villages and in the whole town or the whole city. The most influential races have not only attracted hundreds of thousands of people to participate, but also become the best advertisements to introduce the local areas to the outside world.

各乡镇村落都热衷于举办龙舟赛事，这些赛事规模大小不一，既有村内比赛，也有村与村之间的联合比赛，还有全镇、全市范围的大赛。其中一些影响较大的龙舟赛事不仅在当时吸引了数十万人的参与，更成为当地对外宣传的活广告。

FOSHAN

第二章

龙舟制造 内有玄机

Chapter 2

Dragon Boat Building

不同类型龙舟的制造和装饰各有特点，其速度和使用寿命也各不相同，构成了佛山丰富的龙舟文化。佛山造船巧匠们就是根据代代相传的知识与技艺，结合自己的经验，制作出了一条条迅疾如飞的龙舟。

造龙舟
Dragon Boat Building

Different types of dragon boats have different characteristics in terms of building and decoration, as well as different speeds and service lives, which constitute the rich Foshan dragon boat culture. Dragon boat craftsmen in Foshan have built one fast dragon boat after another by combining the knowledge and skills handed down from generation to generation with their own experience.

2.1 Foshan Dragon Boat Building and Decoration

Although the main structures of dragon boats are basically the same, some boats are fast while others are slow; some are durable with a service life of several decades while others can only be used for a couple of years. Apart from human factors, the building materials, craftsmanship and decorations all play an important role.

Foshan dragon boats have very fastidious requirements of materials, craftsmanship and decorations. In the past, dragon boats were made of hard redwood such as ironwood or Pontianak wood. The latter costs a lot of money. Now, a forty-meter-long dragon boat made of Pontianak wood costs RMB300,000-400,000. The advantage of such a dragon boat is its durability. Even submerged in the mud at the bottom of a creek for a long time, it will not crack or rot. If well-preserved, It can serve up to 7 or 8 decades. The disadvantage is its heavy weight, which slows it down, so it does not have an edge in dragon boat racing. In Foshan, dragon boats are now mostly made of China fir which is easily accessible and inexpensive. For example, the market price of a 32-meter-long dragon boat made of China fir is about RMB100,000. Such dragon boats are light and fast, so they are very popular in dragon boat racing in the Pearl River Delta. But generally, they can only be used for seven to eight years, not as durable as those Pontianak wood ones.

Foshan dragon boats are of various sizes, with the width ranging from 0.66 to 1.32 meters. The wider a dragon boat, the longer it is. In the past, the shortest Foshan dragon boat was about 6 to 10 meters long, which could just seat a couple of people, while the longest could be more than 40 meters long, carrying dozens of people. At that time, there were not many long dragon boats in Foshan. Most

第一节　佛山龙舟的制造与装饰

龙舟的主体结构基本相同，但是有的龙舟划得快，有的划得慢，有的经久耐用，寿命长达几十年，有的却用不了几年，除了人为因素外，还与龙舟的选材、制作工艺、装饰等密不可分。

佛山龙舟无论是选材，还是具体的制作工艺和装饰都大有讲究。以前是用东京格木或坤甸木等坚硬红木制造，坤甸木价格不菲，现在一艘长40米左右的坤甸木龙舟造价要三四十万元。坤甸木龙舟的优点是经久耐用，将之沉进河涌淤泥中，不开裂不腐烂，可以保存较长时间，保存得好的话可以有七八十年的寿命，缺点是比较笨重，划不快，在龙舟竞渡中不占优势。现在佛山造龙舟大都选用杉木，材料易得，造价便宜，一艘长32米的杉木龙舟，市价十万元左右。杉木龙舟去水快，划起来也轻快，在珠三角龙舟竞渡中非常受欢迎，但是杉木龙舟不及坤甸木龙舟耐用，一般只能用七八年。

佛山龙船大小没有定规，身阔二尺许至四尺左右，身窄者则短，身阔者则长。旧时佛山龙舟短者两三丈，可坐数人，长者十余丈，可坐数十人。以前佛山长龙不多，大多长仅三五丈，少数长龙有十来丈。其原因有三：一是佛山很多内河河涌狭窄弯曲，长龙在

转弯的地方需要掘涌砍树方可通行，实在不方便；二是制造长龙的费用为短龙的数倍，经济上也是个负担；三是龙舟越长，其制作技艺要求也越高，否则龙舟中部容易突起甚至断裂。中华人民共和国成立后，佛山大力兴修水利，一些河涌被疏浚拉直，利于长龙通行，改革开放以来，佛山经济飞速发展，各村经济实力大增，因此现在佛山的长龙越造越长，动辄三四十米的长龙。龙舟越长，扒丁就越多，人多力量大，通常速度也会更快。

在佛山，还有一些专门用于比赛的龙舟，无装饰，窄而短，转动灵活。顺德专门用于比赛的龙舟，俗称龙艇，长度从三四米至十七八米不等，可以坐3人、5人、7人、13人或15人。南海的五人龙，也是比赛专用龙舟，船身短，杉木制造，无龙头、龙尾等装饰，转动非常灵活。三水的比赛龙舟分为大龙、中龙和小龙三种。大龙坐20人以上。中龙坐11人或13人，白坭、金本、高丰等地较多，平时用作运输工具。小龙只坐5人，也称为五人龙，分龙艇和龙梭，龙艇扁平，通称禾艇；龙梭较长，头尖尾窄，划起来速度快，白坭、南边、芦苞、大塘、乐平等地较多。

叠滘龙舟
Diejiao Dragon Boat

of them were only 10 to 16 meters long and only a few could be over 30 meters long. There are three reasons for this. First, many inland creeks in Foshan were narrow and curved, so paddlers on long dragon boats would need to dig water courses and cut down trees to turn around, which was really inconvenient. Second, the cost of a long dragon boat was several times that of a short one, which was also an economic burden. Third, the longer the dragon boat was, the higher skills were required. Otherwise, the middle part of the dragon boat would easily protrude or even break. Since the founding of the People's Republic of China, water conservancy projects have been carried out vigorously in Foshan. Creeks have been dredged and straightened to facilitate the passage of long dragon boats. Since the implementation of the reform and opening up policy, the rapid economic development in Foshan has greatly boosted the economic strength of each village. Therefore, Foshan dragon boats have become longer and longer, with a normal length of 30 to 40 meters. The longer the boat, the more paddlers are required, and thus the more powerful and faster it becomes.

In Foshan, there are also a number of undecorated, narrow, short and flexible dragon boats specially designed for racing. In Shunde District, the dragon boats used especially for racing are commonly known as "Longting", with the length ranging from three or four meters to 17 or 18 meters, which can seat three, five, seven, thirteen or fifteen people. In Nanhai District, the five-people dragon boat is also specially made for racing. It has a short body made of China fir with no dragon head, tail or other decorations so that it can move and turn flexibly.

In Sanshui District, the dragon boats for racing are divided into three types: large, medium and small ones. Large dragon boats carry more than 20 people and medium ones 11 or 13 people. They are more popular in towns like Baini, Jinben and Gaofeng, and usually used as a means of transportation in non-racing seasons. Small dragon boats can only seat 5 people, also known as five-people dragon boats. They are divided into two types: "Longting" and "Longsuo". "Longting" is flat, also called "rice boat". "Longsuo" is longer, with a pointed bow and a narrow stern. The latter is fast and more popular in towns such as Baini, Nanbian, Lubao, Datang and Leping.

The main structure of a Foshan dragon boat, from the bottom to the top, includes the bottom board, the keel, the sideboards, the dragon tendons, front and back flag stands, and the seat plates. The keel is joined together with three thick wooden boards. It is like the backbone, supporting the whole dragon boat. The bottom board is attached to the keel. The sideboards must have a smooth surface and the seams must be sealed tightly to prevent leakage. Otherwise the stability and the speed of the dragon boat will be affected. The dragon tendons, the core of the boat, refer to three square wooden boards joined together throughout the whole dragon boat. No matter how long the dragon boat is, the dragon tendons are divided into three sections to increase the boat's elasticity and flexibility. The two joints of the dragon tendons, which control the overall tightness and the level of the bow and the stern must be carefully adjusted so that the rail is neither too loose nor too tight. The front and back flag stands are for holding the flags. The seat plates, which are perpendicular to the dragon tendons, are seats for the paddlers.

The head of a traditional Foshan dragon boat is very majestic, with bright round popping eyes, high horns, a wide open mouth, and a red, black or white beard. Each and every dragon head has its own characteristics due to the time of the construction and the village that builds it. It is usually carved from a whole piece of camphor wood, which is moderately hard and easy to carve. At the same time, camphor wood is insect resistant with its unique fragrance and it is not easy to crack. The Guans in Sanshui District have made some dragon boat heads with sandalwood, which is durable with a unique insect resistant fragrance.

佛山龙舟船身的主要结构由下而上为龙底、龙骨、大旁、龙筋、前后旗盘、坐盘等。龙骨由三块厚实的木板拼接起来，它就像龙舟的脊骨，支撑起整条龙舟。龙底即龙舟底板，底板附着于龙骨上，大旁是龙舟两旁的木板，这些地方接缝要严密，不能漏水，表面必须光滑，否则也会影响龙舟的稳定性和赛龙速度。龙筋是整条船的核心，它是贯通整条龙舟的三根前后相接的方木。不管龙舟长度多少，龙筋都会分为三节，这有助于增加龙舟的柔韧度和灵活度。扎龙筋其实就是调整三节间的两个接头位，这两个位置控制龙舟整体的松紧及龙舟头尾的高低，龙筋必须扎得不松不紧。前后旗盘为插龙船旗的地方，坐盘与龙筋呈十字交叉，为扒丁扒龙舟时的座位。

佛山传统龙舟的龙头非常威风，眼睛圆凸、目睛炯炯，丫角高翘，张口见舌，下颌装有红、黑或白的胡须。由于每艘龙舟的建造年代、所属村落有别，其龙头又各有特点。龙头材料一般用整块香樟木雕刻，樟木软硬适中，容易雕刻，同时樟木有独特的香味，不易生虫，又不易爆裂。三水关氏制造的部分龙舟龙头采用檀木，不但防虫害，还有一股淡淡的清香，坚固耐用。龙

大江冯氏彩龙龙头
Head of the Fengs' Colorful Dragon of Dajiang

盐步老龙龙船头正面图（大沥镇文化站）
Front View of Head of Yanbu Old Dragon Boat (Dali Township Cultural Station)

头一般漆成金色或红色，金色为主，红色为辅，佛山大部分龙舟龙头都漆成金色，而著名的南海九江忠山飞龙龙头就漆成红色，红彤彤的看上去非常威猛。据村民讲，忠山龙头漆成红色，与京剧中关云长的脸谱颜色一致，意表忠义，因忠山是跟随陈子壮[1]起义失败后返乡的义士组建的，象征着陈子壮及其追随者们的忠勇与义气。传统龙舟胡须以黑色最为常见；白须为年长的象征，只有老龙才可用。有些村落的龙舟与其信仰的神灵有关，如叠滘龙舟的胡须大都是黑色，因它们多在北帝（大庙）处“点睛”，而北帝是黑胡须，龙舟也随之用黑胡须。叠滘陈丰坊、庆云坊（海边坊）龙舟的胡须又别具特色。陈丰坊龙舟在老土地庙“点睛”，而老土地是白胡须，龙舟也随之用白胡须。

1　陈子壮（1596—1647），字集生，号秋涛，广东南海县沙贝乡（今广州白云区）人。与陈邦彦、张家玉自1647年2月起兵，至11月为清军所败，坚持抗击清兵十个月之久。后子壮兵败被俘，宁死不降，受酷刑而死，与战死的陈邦彦、张家玉一起被称为“岭南三忠”。

Generally, most dragon heads are painted gold while some red. Most of Foshan dragon boats have golden heads, but the famous dragon boat named Zhongshan Flying Dragon in Jiujiang Town, Nanhai District has a red head, rendering it very powerful. According to the villagers, the red color is consistent with that of Guan Yu's face in Peking Opera, showing loyalty in that the original boat was made by the followers of Chen Zizhuang [1] after their failed uprising and their return home. The dragon boat signifies the courage and loyalty of Chen and his followers. Traditional dragon heads usually have black beards, while the white ones are the symbol of seniority, and can only be used by old dragon boats. Some villages choose the color based on the gods they believe in. For example, dragon boats in Diejiao mostly have black beards because the eyes of their dragon heads are usually dotted at the Temple of Emperor Xuanwu, who has a black beard. The beards of dragon boats of Chenfengfang and Qingyunfang (Haibianfang) in Diejiao are distinctive. Chenfengfang has the eyes of the dragon heads dotted at the Temple of the Lord of Soil and Ground who has a white beard, so the beards of the dragons boats are also painted white.

The dragon tail, also carved from camphor wood, is usually stored together with the dragon head in ancestral halls or village temples, and will be installed on the dragon boat when there are dragon boat activities. The dragon tail is slightly upward, mostly painted with golden dragon scales, looking fierce and aggressive.

The dragon card, carved with camphor wood and painted red or black, is an essential component on every traditional Foshan dragon boat. It is inserted in the dragon head, marking the name of the dragon boat to let people know which community or village the boat belongs to. Before building a new dragon boat,

1 Chen zizhuang (1596-1647), who styled himself as "Jisheng"or "Qiutao", was born in Shabei Village, Nanhai County, Guangdong Province (now Baiyun District, Guangzhou City, Guangdong Province). Together with Chen Bangyan and Zhang Jiayu, Chen started an uprising in February 1647, fighting against the Qing Dynasty army for ten months, and was defeated in November of the same year. After the defeat, Chen was captured but would rather die than surrender. Then he died from cruel torture. Chen Zizhuang, Chen Bangyan and Zhang Jiayu, the latter two killed in the battle field, are known as the "Lingnan Sanzhong"(three loyal generals from Lingnan).

九江传统龙舟龙牌
Traditional Dragon Boat Cards of Jiujiang

the dragon boat club must agree on its name, which is generally combined with names of the place and the god worshiped in the village temple. To name the dragon boat after the god of the temple, the villagers need to pray for permission of the god. Dragon boats are named after the villages if they don't have their own village temples. In recent years, with the prosperity of the Foshan dragon boat culture, some enterprises and associations have also built dragon boats. These boats do not belong to any village temple or village, so they cannot be named in the same pattern, but the name, which should convey auspicious meanings. After the name is determined, the dragon boat club will have the dragon boat tailor-made at a dragon boatyard.

Paddles need light materials. In the past, citrus medica was mostly used. The weight of each paddle was no more than one kilogram. Nowadays, carbon fiber is more widely used because of its lightness and handiness. According to some local people, before the founding of the People's Republic of China, because disputes often occurred during dragon boat racing, iron paddles could be used as weapons at any time.

The dragon boat drum is usually placed behind the special umbrellas. If the dragon boat is too long, the drum will be placed in the middle. It is the soul of each boat, because it gives orders to control the speed, draws the paddlers' attention to pass waters of different situations and carries out various dragon boat etiquettes. The beats of the dragon boat drum in Jiujiang Town, Nanhai District are very special. They are divided into one-, three-, and seven-beat rhythms,

龙尾也用樟木雕刻而成，平时和龙头一起被放在祠堂或社庙中，龙舟活动时才会装上龙舟。龙尾稍微向上卷，上面大都绘有金色的龙鳞，显得凶狠好斗。

龙牌是每一艘佛山传统龙舟的必备之物，插在龙头部位，标注着该龙舟的名字，让人一见就知道是哪社哪村的龙舟。龙牌由樟木雕刻而成，漆成红色或黑色。在制造一条新龙舟前，龙船会须先商定龙舟的名称。龙舟的名称一般由龙舟所在地地名和社庙庙宇供奉的神祇名合成，要以庙宇神祇命名，需先去庙宇求神问卜，征得神祇的同意。有些村落没有社庙，就以地名来命名。近年来，随着佛山龙舟文化的兴盛，一些企业、协会等也制造了龙舟，这些龙舟不属于任何社庙或村落，所以命名不能用以上的方法，但要取个“好意头”。龙舟的名称确定后，龙船会就着手去龙舟制造厂订造龙舟。

船桨，需要用轻便的材料，以前多用椽木，每只桡的重量不超过一千克。现在多用碳纤维，更加轻便好用。采访中有当地人指出，中华人民共和国成立前有用铁桡的，因为那时龙舟竞渡经常起纠纷，铁桡可以随时当作武器使用。

大江冯氏彩龙龙船鼓，要两个人擂鼓
Drum of the Fengs' Colorful Dragon Boat of Dajiang, Two Drummers Required

龙船鼓通常置于罗伞后面，若龙舟比较长，鼓就置于龙舟中部。龙船鼓是每一条船的灵魂，它指挥龙船的前进速度、提示路过不同情况的水域和施行各种龙舟礼仪。南海九江的龙船鼓点很特别，分一声、三声、七声三种，不同的鼓点有不同的意义。过桥、转弯的时候都是敲一声鼓。过桥时敲比较急速的一声鼓，一声鼓点扒一下桨，扒丁们低头弯腰拼命划桨，扒丁们的呐喊声和“咚咚咚”的鼓声交织在一起，鼓舞扒丁们一鼓作气冲过桥底。转弯的时候也是敲一声鼓，九江很多河涌都是弯曲狭窄的，有些弯比较急，如果扒丁一直扒下去，船头掌舵的人可能来不及转舵，这时鼓手就要根据入弯的情况，用节奏快的一声鼓连续打，意思是叫扒丁停扒。扒老龙也是敲一声鼓，“咚、咚、咚”一下一下沉闷而规律的鼓声，显出老龙的老态和稳重。九江以前赛龙都是敲三声鼓，现在赛龙多敲一声鼓，因为一声鼓简单且韵律感强，一声、三声鼓都是九江年轻人平常最喜欢打的。七声鼓的主旋律与三声鼓相仿，但七声鼓敲七个鼓点才落一次扒，因此速度比较慢，通常在与阿契（即兄弟）相遇、阿契放炮仗、送高标和龙舟靠岸时用到。七声鼓比较难，现在只有五六十岁以上的人才会打、会听。

九江沙滘侯王罗伞
Marquis Prince Umbrella of Shajiao, Jiujiang

佛山龙舟上都有装饰。在龙舟活动中，龙舟不仅要斗速，还要斗靓，不仅有赛龙斗标，还有彩龙竞艳。赛龙的装饰比较简单，一般只有龙牌、

which have different meanings. One-beat rhythm means crossing the bridge or turning. When crossing the bridge, paddlers will hear rapid one-beat rhythm and paddle very hard according to the beat of the drum. With the paddlers' shouts and thunderous drumbeats, the dragon boat rushes across the bridge. When turning, paddlers will also hear one-beat rhythm. In Jiujiang Town, many creeks are curved and narrow. At some of the sharp curves, if paddlers keep paddling, the steersman may not have enough time to turn the rudder. So, according to the situation of the turning, the drummer keeps the rapid one-beat rhythm to stop paddlers from paddling. Drummers on old dragon boats also use one-beat rhythm. The deep and regular drumbeats show the seniority and dignity of the old dragon boats. In the past, the dragon boat races in Jiujiang Town usually used three-beat rhythm, but now mostly one-beat one because of its simplicity and strong rhythm. One- and three-beat rhythms are both popular among young people in Jiujiang Town. The cadence of the seven-beat rhythm is similar to that of the three-beat one. But the seven-beat one means the paddlers only paddle once every seven beats, so the speed is very slow. It is usually used when meeting sworn brothers, sworn brothers setting off firecrackers, sending "Gaobiao" (a bamboo pole carrying a piece of colored cloth) and docking the dragon boat. It is difficult to play the seven-beat rhythm, which can now only be played and followed by people over 50 or 60 years old.

Most Foshan dragon boats have decorations. In dragon boat activities, they compete in terms of both speed and decorations. The decorations of the dragon boat for racing are relatively simple, usually just with the dragon card and the dragon boat drum, and some even without decorations. But the decorations of the dragon boat for a beauty contest are more complicated.

When the colorful dragon boats cruise, their decorations mainly include the dragon card, the dragon boat drum, the special umbrellas, the gong, the bow flag, the commanding flag, the stern flag and so on. The special umbrellas are usually placed in the front and back of the dragon boat, behind the dragon card and in front of the gong. The patterns on the special umbrellas used to be Guan Yu, but now, the cloud dragon, phoenix, lion, eight immortals, peony, plum flower and other auspicious patterns are more popular. In the old days, the umbrellas were made by the villagers who were good at needlework. These hand-embroidered umbrellas were very beautiful with exquisite workmanship. Now, they are mostly bought outside. According to the old people, during the Guangxu period (1871-1908) of the Qing Dynasty, there was a dragon boat named "Zhongzhou" in the Beijiang River in Nanhai District. Mr. Zhu, the person holding the umbrella on this boat had amazingly strong arms that he could turn the umbrella like a windmill easily for half an hour on end, making the whole dragon boat look mighty and vigorous and all the audience cheer in amazement.

华伞

Special Umbrellas

The gong is usually placed at the back of the dragon boat. Hitting the gong also requires techniques. There is a legend of the so-called “Zhongshan Gong” in Jiujiang Town, Nanhai District. In the Qing Dynasty (1644–1912), a man named Chen Li, born in Jiujiang, was a skilled gong player on the "Zhongshan" dragon boat. When the boat was crossing the place now known as the Sanyuan Bridge at the Chuanlan Street in Rulin Community, Chen was able to throw the gong up over the bridge and catch it after the dragon boat had crossed the bridge. He had performed this many times without failures, which earned him huge reputation. However, the stunt of "flying the gong over the bridge" has been lost.

On both sides of the dragon card are inserted the bow flags, usually with couplets written on them. Jiujiang dragon boats have the tradition of making sworn brothers and each group has its own couplets. For example, the couplets of General Zhou (Zhou Yafu, a famous general of the western Han Dynasty) and its sworn brothers mention their friendship with each other while those of Yanbu Old Dragon refer to its past win in the racing and its ties with Pantang Dragon Boat.

龙船鼓，有的甚至无任何装饰，彩龙的装饰比赛龙复杂。

彩龙巡游时，龙舟上的装饰物主要有龙牌、龙船鼓、罗伞、铜锣、船头旗、帅旗、船尾旗等。罗伞通常放在龙舟的前后，在龙牌之后、铜锣之前。罗伞图案，以前多用关公，现在用云龙、凤鸟、狮子、八仙、牡丹、梅花等吉祥图案。旧时罗伞都是由村中会女红的村民制作，手工刺绣，做工精美；现在都是在外面购买。据老人回忆，清光绪年间，南海北江有一条名叫“中洲”的龙舟，掌伞者姓朱，臂力惊人，他以灵活的双臂，轻松自如地将罗伞转动得如风车般，且每次能持续半小时之久，使整艘龙舟显得威猛又有活力，观者无不喝彩叫绝。

彩龙巡游
Cruise of Colorful Dragon Boats

铜锣一般置于龙舟尾部。敲铜锣也是个技术活，南海九江有所谓“忠山锣”的传奇。清代有一位名叫陈礼的九江人，为忠山龙船锣手，技艺高超，当龙舟过今儒林社区船栏街三元桥时，他能将所敲的铜锣抛高数丈，掷过三元桥顶，待龙舟穿过桥底后又用手接住，来回表演多次，从未失手，因而名声大噪，可惜“飞锣过桥”绝技现已失传。

龙牌两侧会插上船头旗，旗上通常都书写对联。九江传统龙舟有结契的传统，每一帮阿契都有自己的对联，周将军（西汉名将周亚夫）与其契友的对联以前是“弄笛升平七友至，吹箫能引九龙飞”，现在是“弄笛升平群友至，吹箫能引锦龙飞”。南海区盐步老龙的对联为“昔日夺标同鼎甲，当年沧海占群龙”和“昔日夺标同结契，当年沧海冠群龙”。

帅旗即本村落的标志旗，插在鼓的后方，形状不一，有三角旗，也有长方形旗；色彩缤纷，有红色、黄色、黑色，也有彩色等。人们远远看到这些形状和颜色独具特点的帅旗，就能知道此龙舟属于哪个村落。南海九江传统龙舟帅旗的背面比较特别，会画上关帝像，这与九江人将关公当成水神加以崇拜有关。

船尾旗有白色、黑色、彩色之分，不同的龙舟会插不同的船尾旗，暗示该村信奉哪位水神，如黑色的七星旗代表信奉北帝，白色的七星旗代表信奉观音。还有黑布镶白边的七星旗也是传统的船尾旗。现在一些龙舟使用彩色船尾旗，更加鲜艳夺目。

佛山顺德等地的龙舟上还有一个重要部分——神楼（船舱中的小神龛），神楼里供奉的是社庙神灵的“行宫”，其“坐宫”一直被供奉在庙中，在村中有大事或者需要请神出游时，就会请出神的“行宫”。“行宫”前要点燃三支香烛，有的供奉关帝，有的供奉天后，有的供奉洪圣大王，还有的供奉北帝，这都根据村中社庙供奉的神灵而定。

The commanding flag is the symbol of the village, inserted behind the drum. The flags are of various shapes such as triangular and rectangular, and of different colors including red, yellow, black, and multicolor. People can tell which village the dragon boat belongs to as soon as they see those commanding flags with distinctive shapes and colors. The back of the commanding flag on a traditional dragon boat in Jiujiang Town, Nanhai District is very special, painted with the image of Guan Yu, which is closely related to Jiujiang people's worship of Guan Yu as the water god.

龙牌
Dragon Boat Card

The stern flag is also of different colors including white, black or multicolor. Different dragon boats have different stern flags, indicating which water god the village worships. For example, the black seven-star flag represents belief in Emperor Xuanwu, and the white seven-star flag in Guanyin. The black seven-star flag with white border is also a traditional stern flag. Now some dragon boats use multicolored stern flags, which are more eye-catching.

There is also an important component of the dragon boat in Shunde District, Foshan City and other places - the God Building, which houses the traveling statue of the god of the village temple. The sitting statue of the god is enshrined in the temple all the time, while the traveling statue of the god is invited out when there is a big event in the village or the necessity for the god to travel. Three joss sticks should be lit in front of the traveling statues of the gods. The gods worshiped include Guan Yu, the Queen of Heaven, King Hongsheng, Emperor Xuanwu and so on, the same as the gods worshiped in each village temple.

2.2 Foshan Boatyards and Boat Builders

In the past, dragon boat activities were prosperous in Foshan. Skillful boat builders could be found in many villages. However, skills of building dragon boats have been lost in some villages as time goes by. At present, there are a few dragon boat manufacturers in Foshan. Among them, the Guans Dragon Boat Manufacturer in Xinsha Village and Li Bao'an Dragon Boat Manufacturer in Zhoubian Village, both in Sanshui District of Foshan City, are two famous ones throughout the Pearl River Delta. In 2013, the Guans' skill of building dragon boats was included in the list of representative items of intangible cultural heritages in Foshan; so was Li Bao'an's skill of building dragon boats in 2017.

The Guan family has been building dragon boats for generations. In recent years, racers who have used dragon boats made by them have won prizes for many times in dragon boat races at home and abroad. For instance, in the 7th Asian Arts Festival, the dragon boats used by the top three winners in the race were all made by the Guan family; in the 16th "Lotus Cup" Dragon Boat Race hosted in Panyu District of Guangzhou City in 2017, the top three winners won with the dragon boats made by the Guans too. In addition, their dragon boats have been sold to California, US.

In April 2018, The author visited the Guans Dragon Boat Manufacturer which is situated in Xinsha Village in the Southwest Street of Sanshui District, out of admiration for the legendary master builders of dragon boats. Xinsha Village is located on an old sandy island along the Beijiang River. It is said that 95% of the local residents started to make a living by building boats since the 19th century. Yet the vast majority of them have quit in recent years because of diminishing demand for wooden boats, and only the Guan family has turned to building

第二节　佛山造船工厂和造船巧匠

旧时佛山龙舟活动兴盛，很多村落都有龙舟制造巧匠，随着时间的推移，一些村落造龙舟的技艺逐渐失传。目前，在佛山还有数家龙舟制造厂，如闻名于珠三角的三水新沙村关氏造船厂、三水洲边村李保安龙船制造厂。2013年关家的龙舟制作技艺被评为佛山市非物质文化遗产代表性项目，2017年李保安龙舟制造技艺也被评为市级非遗项目。

关氏家族世代制作龙舟，近年来他们制作的龙舟多次获得国内外龙舟赛事的大奖：在第七届亚洲艺术节龙舟赛事上获得前三名的龙舟都是出自关氏家族之手；2017年广州市番禺区第十六届“莲花杯”龙舟赛，前三名全部被关家制造的龙舟夺得。他们制造的龙舟还曾远涉重洋，销往美国加州。

关氏造船厂内景

Inner Scene of the Guans Dragon Boat Manufacturer

2018年4月的暮春时节，笔者慕名来到三水区西南街道新沙村关氏造船厂，探访传说中的造船高人。新沙村位于北江边的老沙岛上，据说从19世纪开始，岛上居民就以造船为业，95%人家都是造船的。近年来，随着木船需求的减少，绝大多数居民已经不再造船，只有关家转型造龙舟。

目前关氏造船厂挑大梁的是关勇强、关永强兄弟俩，但关家造船的家史可追溯到上几辈。据兄弟俩的父亲关苏所言，早在其高祖父那一辈，关家就开了造船厂，各种船只都会做。后来他的曾祖父又去芦苞开船厂，祖父曾在河口开船厂。中华人民共和国成立后，国家实行公私合营政策，关家的船厂并入国营造船厂，父亲关队也进入国营新沙造船厂工作。出生于造船世家的关队，在厂里是技术一把手，从设计到制作，全都由他监管。从渔家小艇到运砂货船，关队造船无数，但他最牵挂的还是造龙舟。20世纪80年代，他从造船厂退休，遂与人合伙造龙舟。20世纪90年代，他独自开办了龙船厂，因技术精湛、经营有方，生意越来越红火。2000年前后，关队将龙船厂交给了儿子关苏，自己退居幕后，平时在家雕刻龙头、龙尾，悠闲自在，2011年，80多岁的关队去世。

关苏自幼对龙舟非常感兴趣，喜爱看龙舟竞渡，成年后进入广州一家造船厂工作，后来船厂不景气，他下岗了，就回到三水跟父亲一起造龙舟。2000年前后，关苏从父亲手中接过造船厂，带领双胞胎儿子继续造龙舟。2017年12月，关苏成为佛山市第五批市级非遗项目龙舟制造技艺传承人。

据关苏介绍，以前造龙舟，大都选择坤甸木等硬木，坚固耐用，但是船身比较笨重，划起来速度不快。20世纪80年代以来，随

dragon boats.

Today, it is Guan Yongqiang and his twin brother Guan Yongqiang (the "Yong" characters in their names are different in Chinese) who play the leading role in the manufacturer. In fact, the Guan family has built boats for generations. According to Guan Su, the father of the twin brothers, the history of the family boatyard dates back to his great great grandfather's lifetime, and all kinds of boats could be made in the boatyard. Afterwards, his great grandfather set up a new boatyard in Lubao Town, and then his grandfather set up a new boatyard in Hekou Town. After the founding of the People's Republic of China, the Chinese government implemented the policy of public-private partnership, so the Guan family boatyard was merged into the Xinsha State-Owned Shipyard, and Guan Dui, Guan Su's father, began to work there as a technical director in charge of work from design to manufacture. Although he had built various kinds of boats from fishermen's boats to freighters carrying sand, dragon boats were Guan Dui's favorite. In the 1980s, he retired from the shipyard and then began to build dragon boats in partnership with other people. In the 1990s, he set up his own dragon boat manufacturer and the business became more and more flourishing as a result of his superb techniques and good management. Around 2000, Guan Dui took the back seat by handing the manufacturer over to his son Guan Su. After retirement, he liked to carve dragon heads and tails, living a comfortable life until 2011 when he passed away in his 80s.

Guan Su has been very interested in dragon boats and fond of watching dragon boat racing since childhood. He found a job in a boat manufacturer in Guangzhou after coming of age. But he was laid off when it witnessed a downturn in business. Thus, he returned to Sanshui and followed his father to build dragon boats. Around 2000, Guan Su inherited his family boatyard from his father and continued to build dragon boats with his twin sons. In December 2017, Guan Su was chosen as one of the fifth batch of intangible cultural heritages inheritors in tems of dragon boat building skills in Foshan.

According to Guan Su, dragon boat builders used to choose hardwood like Pontianak wood to make dragon boats because of its sturdiness and durability. But such dragon boats are heavy and thus move slowly. With the development of dragon boat racing since the 1980s, boat builders have been inclined to select China fir rather than Pontianak wood as materials. Having strict standards of wood selection, the Guan family always selects superior China fir in the remote mountains of Guizhou Province and Guangxi Zhuang Autonomous Region. Firstly, the wood must contain adequate fiber and be light and evenly distributed. Dragon boats made of China fir have smooth surface to reduce water resistance, and can help racers to get good results. Secondly, the wood must be at least 18 centimeters in diameter and the longer, the better. That's because boat builders don't need to splice boards if the diameter is long enough. Lastly and the most importantly, the China fir wood must be straight and big so that three pieces can be spliced together as the keel. After selecting the keel, boat builders will hold a ceremony on an auspicious day to start making a dragon boat. During the ceremony, they will lay out offerings, light the joss sticks and candles, set off firecrackers, worship the gods and ancestors and then write down the name of the buyer—named after the village, company or association—on the surface of the keel.

After the ceremony, the making of the dragon boat begins. It is very complicated to make a dragon boat. The major procedures include making the keel, nailing the butterfly chassis, bending the keel to make it streamlined, determining the midline, installing flaps, installing the sideboards, making the rungs, making the seat boards, installing the dragon tendons, reinforcing the seat boards and the dragon tendons with bamboo chips, polishing, painting, and making and installing the dragon head and tail. Each procedure must be taken seriously because a simple error can affect the performance of the dragon boat. In the past, all procedures had to be finished manually, so it usually took four people a month to build a dragon boat. But since the 1980s, an innovative way of semi-mechanization and assembly line work has been established so cutting materials, hammering nails, polishing the hull and some other procedures could be done by machines. As a result, four boat builders working together are able to build three dragon boats in a month, which means that one takes about ten days on average. During the process, hand tools used include adzes, chisels, planes, saws, drills, carpenter's ink markers, level gauges and all kinds of rulers; mechanical devices

着龙舟竞技运动的发展，人们不再做坤甸木龙舟，都是造杉木龙舟。关家龙舟选材严格，都是选择来自贵州、广西深山的上好杉木，木头要有足够的纤维、匀称轻巧，这种木材造出来的龙舟表面光滑，在水中行进时受到的阻力小，在比赛中就能获得好成绩。木材直径至少要18厘米，直径越大越好，足够大的话就可以省去拼板的工序。底骨（龙骨）的选择最为重要，必须选择笔直的大杉木，三根杉木拼接成一根底骨。底骨选好后，会选一个好日子举行开工仪式，摆上供品，燃烧香烛鞭炮，拜神，然后在底骨上写上订船方的名字，如某村、某公司、某协会。

开工仪式过后，龙舟制作就正式开始了。制作一条龙舟的工艺非常复杂，主要工序有做底骨、起底、起水、打水平、转水、装大旁、做横挡、做坐板、安龙筋、用竹片加固坐板与龙筋、打磨、刷漆、制作安装龙头与龙尾。每一道工艺都必须小心谨慎，任何一步没有到位，都会影响龙舟的性能。以前全部工序都要靠人工来完成，因此速度比较慢，四个人合作一个月才能造一条龙舟。20世纪80年代以后，切割材料、钉钉子、为船身打磨等工序可以用机械代劳，形成了半机械化和流水线作业，一般四个人合作一个月可以造出三条龙舟，一条龙舟平均耗时十天左右。使用的手工工具有锛、凿、刨、锯、钻、墨斗、水平仪、各种尺子，机械有电锯、电动打磨机、充气钻等。水平仪是在制作龙舟过程中频繁使用的工具，几乎每一道流程的前后都要用到，只有这样才能保证龙舟在水中快速前进时的稳定性。

笔者在工棚中亲眼目睹了关苏师傅为龙底打水平的过程。地面

关苏师傅在为底骨打墨线
Master Guan Inking the Midline of the Keel

上每隔一米竖立一个船桩，数十个船桩排成整齐的一长排，中间低两端逐渐升高，长达三四十米的龙舟底骨固定在木桩上，形成一定的弧度。用水平仪确定整条底骨的中线是非常关键的步骤，这条中线不仅是龙骨的中线，也将是整条龙舟的中线，中线定准了，船才能保持平衡。只见关师傅走到底骨一侧，闭起一只眼睛仔细测量，每间隔一米左右就用水平仪定出一个中点，然后用墨线将两个中点连起来，不断重复这套程序，直至将整条龙舟的中线定位好。关师傅是整个龙船厂的技术总监，所有关键工序都由他把关。打水平之后，还要装底板、装大旁、安龙筋等，这些工序都很重要，其比例和弧度都要非常精确，这样龙舟才能在水中平稳快速行驶。正是这种严格选材和精雕细刻的工匠精神，使得关家造出来的龙舟速度够快、经久耐用，成就了关家龙舟在珠三角乃至国外的好名声，甚至不少人愿意加价1万~2万元请关家制造龙舟。

关苏介绍，拼板也是一个技术活。一条龙舟是由多块木板拼成，龙骨和龙筋也是由木板拼接成。拼接木板时，木板之间不需要任何黏合剂，但需要将结合处打磨得非常光滑，使得木板与木板拼接在一起能严丝合缝，这样龙舟才不会进水。为了使龙舟更稳定，

include electric saws, electric grinders, pneumatic drills and others. Among them, level gauges are the most frequently used since they are required before and after nearly each procedure. Only in this way can boat builders guarantee the stability of the dragon boat when it is moving fast in the water.

The author was lucky to see how master Guan Su determined the midline in his work shed. There was a long and straight line of a dozen ship piles erected at an interval of one meter on the ground, low in the middle and gradually rising at both ends. The keel of thirty to forty meters was fixed to the piles, forming a certain curve. Then came the most crucial part—to determine the midline of the keel with the level gauge. Correct determination of the midline keeps the balance of a dragon boat. Master Guan Su stepped to one side of the keel; next, he carefully measured it up with one eye closed and set a midpoint with a level gauge every meter; then, he joined the adjacent midpoints with an inked line and kept repeating this procedure until the midline of the keel was determined. Master Guan Su was the technical director in the manufacturer, whose duty was to check on all crucial procedures such as determining the midline, and installing the chassis, sideboards and dragon tendons.

The ratios and radians required in each procedure must be handled accurately so that the dragon boat can move quickly and steadily in the water. It is this craftsmanship involving strict wood selection and meticulous carving that has helped the Guan family to build fast and durable dragon boats and has contributed to their good reputation all over the Pearl River Delta and even the rest of the world. As a result, many people are willing to pay an extra sum of RMB10,000-20,000 in order to ask the Guan family to build dragon boats for them.

两位师傅在起底

Two Master Workers Nailing the Butterfly Chassis

According to Guan Su, splicing boards also requires techniques. A dragon boat is put together with several boards and so are the keel and the dragon tendons. Adhesives are not required in the process of splicing boards, but joints of the boards need to be polished well so that they can be spliced together perfectly to prevent leakage. In order to make the dragon boat steadier, a large number of nails need to be hammered into the joints of the chassis, the sideboards and the rungs. Yet the nails cannot be hammered all the way through those boards. Otherwise, the boat will leak. Boat builders usually punch a hole with a pneumatic drill before hammering a nail. The outside of each nail is smoothed with polyurethane to make the dragon boat waterproof and smoother.

There are high seasons and low seasons for dragon boat building. Every year, the low season is from the Dragon Boat Festival to the tenth lunar month. During this period, boat builders will go to watch dragon boat races from place to place, to observe the performance of their boats and learn about the advantages of other people's boats. In doing so, they make preparations for the improvement of their dragon boats next year. The high season is the rest of the time, spanning from the tenth lunar month of a year to the Dragon Boat Festival next year. In particular, boat builders are much busier during the one or two months before the Dragon Boat Festival. To speed up making dragon boats, boat builders work from around 7 a.m. to 9 p.m. They only have a short rest at mealtimes. In spite of a tight schedule, the Guans still maintain the strict standard of each procedure. They guard their reputation and their love for dragon boats by staying true to the craftsmanship. This spirit is embodied in not only the emphasis on each procedure but also the strict control of the number of orders. In 2018, the Guan family received 40-plus orders from Guangzhou, Dongguan, Kaiping and some other places. But in the end, they only accepted 30-plus of them due to a limited workshop and a tight schedule.

As their grandfather Guang Dui passed away and their father Guan Su is getting older, the twin brothers begin to play the leading role in the Guans' manufacturer. They were once taxi drivers in Guangzhou. Since competition in the taxi industry became fiercer almost 20 years ago, they decided to change their jobs and went back to Sanshui successively to learn building dragon boats

在龙骨与底板、横挡与大旁结合处，都需要钉大量的钉子。钉钉子时不能把木板打穿，否则会进水。每钉一根钉子，都是先用充气钻打洞，再把钉子插进去。每根钉子的外部都要用聚氨酯抹平，既防水又能让船身更平滑。

关永强、关勇强兄弟俩安装龙舟坐板
The Guans' Twin Brothers Installing the Seat Plates of the Dragon Boat

造龙舟有淡季和旺季之分。淡季为每年端午节到农历十月，这段时间他们去各地看龙舟赛，了解自己制作的龙舟在比赛中的表现，并学习其他龙舟的优势，为来年的龙舟改良做准备。农历十月到来年的端午节前这段时间就是旺季，尤其是临近端午节前的一两个月会更忙。为了赶制龙舟，匠人们每天早上7点多就开工，一直忙到晚上9点，中间只有吃饭的时间休息一会儿。尽管时间很紧，但关家并没有因此降低对工艺的要求，他们用工匠精神守护自己的声誉和龙舟情怀。这种工匠精神不仅体现在重视制作工艺上，还体现在严格控制接订单的数量上。2018年关家接到了来自广州、东莞、开平等地40多条龙舟订单，但因为厂房小、时间紧，他们拒绝了10多条龙舟订单，只接了30多条龙舟订单。

随着祖父关队的去世、父亲关苏的日渐老去，关家造船厂挑大梁的任务传到了关勇强、关永强兄弟俩身上。兄弟两人为双胞胎，原在广州开出租车，后来由于出租车行业竞争越来越激烈，兄弟俩决定改行，先后回到三水跟爷爷和父亲学造龙舟，至今快20年了。据关永强透露，兄弟俩刚开始学时非常艰难，每天十几个小时围着龙舟转，沉闷无聊；刨木板、测量、钉钉子、涂防水胶、打磨……大部分都是手工操作，他们累得腰酸背疼，手也磨出了厚茧，比开出租车辛苦多了。他们制作龙舟都是根据客户的要求定制，龙骨的弧度，龙舟的流线型，龙头、龙尾部分的收束，都没有定规，需要依靠平常的经验积累。即使有爷爷的耐心教导，初学的兄弟俩仍然面临着极大的挑战。他们当时就想着硬着头皮熬一段时间，找到了其他更好的职业就改行，根本没想会干一辈子。兄弟俩心不在焉的态度让爷爷很不满，导致两人天天挨骂。经过时光的打磨，加上爷爷、父亲的悉心传授和严格要求，兄弟俩的技艺日渐长进，一两年后就基本掌握了造龙舟的全套工序，现在早已经挑起了关氏龙舟的大梁。

造龙舟是个细致活，从最初的选料到最后刷漆、调试，每一道工序都有着严格的要求，一道工序没有做好，就会影响龙舟的性能。加之每一艘龙舟都是客户定制的，其要求和尺寸都不相同，因此在造龙舟之前，要选好合适的木材，然后精心设计，精密计算各部位的尺寸。兄弟俩秉承着家训，用心制造龙舟。他们备有数个笔记本，专门记录他们制造的龙舟的各部位尺寸，检测其是否符合设计要求。做好之后还要进行调试，以保证龙舟呈现出最好的状态。为了适应现代龙舟比赛的需要，关氏兄弟也在不断地探索创新，但为了保险，每年只是改进一点点。比如关家制造的龙舟头部都是三

from their grandfather and father. The younger brother tells the author that they found it very difficult to build a dragon boat when they just started learning. For one thing, they were bored with working around the dragon boat for a dozen hours every day. For another, they were exhausted and their hands even developed thick calluses because most of the jobs were done manually, such as planing boards, measuring, hammering nails, applying the waterproof glue and polishing, which made them think that being a boat builder was more laborious than being a taxi driver. In addition, they made dragon boats in accordance with customers' requirements, which means there are no set rules for making each boat, so they had to depend on accumulated experience to set the standard for the radian of the keel, the streamlining of the dragon boat and the restraints of the dragon head and tail. Even with their grandfather's patient instructions, the two beginners were still confronted with great challenges. They originally planned to bite the bullet until they found better jobs, since they didn't expect to make dragon boats forever. However, the absent-minded attitude of the two brothers made their grandfather very dissatisfied, and consequently they were scolded every day. With the careful instructions and strict requirements of their grandfather and father, they made progress in the skills day by day and mastered the whole process of building a dragon boat in just one to two years. Now they have already become the mainstay of the Guans' dragon boat business.

Building a dragon boat is a painstaking job. Strict standards are set for all procedures from wood selection to polishing and adjustment. Even a simple error can influence the performance of a dragon boat. What's more, different customers have different requirements, so boat builders must select suitable wood and make accurate calculations for the size of each part of a dragon boat. The twin brothers, committed to their family motto, are devoted to building dragon boats. They prepare several notebooks specifically to record all the measurements of their dragon boats and check whether they meet the design requirements. A dragon boat needs adjustment after it is finished to ensure that it is in its best state. To meet the needs of modern dragon boat races, they keep innovating, but only improve a little bit every year as insurance. For example, dragon boats made by the Guan family have triangular heads, which can reduce water resistance, and before long they are copied by many other dragon boat manufacturers. Another innovative example is that the hull of their dragon boats is made narrower, from 1.48m and 1.38m to 1.18m to even 1.03m. A narrower hull means a shallower draught. Thus, the dragon boat can move faster. Yet, the younger brother mentions that although with the above advantages, the stability declines. It's hard to strike a balance. Apart from that innovation, they also move the drum forward from the middle of the boat, which improves the paddling condition of the paddlers behind the drum. Usually, paddlers in the middle of a dragon boat are strong young people. Therefore, a little improvement can make a big difference. Besides, they also search the Internet for new techniques of building dragon boats so as to adapt to the development of modern dragon boat races.

Guan Su and his sons point out that a longer dragon boat requires more paddlers and thus moves faster, but is more difficult to build. Normally, a dragon boat is no more than 42 meters long. Beyond this limit, the technique must be improved several times for each additional meter. The longest dragon boat that the Guan family has built is 46.9 meters long. If the dragon head and tail are added, it is over 50 meters long and needs over 90 paddlers to make it move. It was specially designed and made for a dragon boat team in Xipu Village, Fangcun, Guangzhou. The Guan family has also built another dragon boat of the same size for Yayao Community of Dali Town. Nowadays, the dragon boat business of the Guan family has spread throughout the Pearl River Delta and even the rest of the world, and it receives twenty to thirty orders annually in recent years. However, Guan Su and his sons are not so positive about the future of the business and position dragon boat building as a sunset industry. There are two main reasons. One is that it is a laborious job and the return is not high so the younger generation prefer to work in a factory rather than learn how to make dragon boats. Today, the twin brothers, born in 1973, are the youngest dragon boat builders in the manufacturer. Most boat builders are about 60 years old and Guan Su is nearly 70. The other is that the government policies have a great influence on orders for dragon boats. Around 2008, there were many orders, thanks to the holding of the Olympic Games and the Asian Games,

角形的，减少了水的阻力，但后来很快被其他龙舟厂效仿。他们制造的龙舟船身也在不断变窄，1.48米、1.38米、1.18米，甚至达到1.03米，舟身越窄，吃水越少，速度就加快了。关永强还提到，龙舟船身越窄速度越快，但是稳定性就变差了，二者很难兼顾，这是一个难题。现在他们还把中间放龙船鼓的位置往前挪，这样就不会影响到龙船鼓后的扒丁划桨。龙舟中间的扒丁都是力量大的年轻人，一点小小的改进就可以使龙舟更快。他们还上网查找造龙舟的新技术，以适应当代龙舟运动发展的需要。

师傅正在涂防水胶
A Master Worker Applying Waterproof Glue

关于龙舟长度，关氏父子指出，龙舟越长需要的扒丁就越多，速度也越快，但制作的难度也随之增加。一般龙舟的长度不会超过42米，超过这个限度，每增加 1 米，技术工艺要提高几倍。关家制造的最长的龙舟达46.9米，加上龙头、龙尾，长50多米，需要90多人才能划动，是前几年为广州芳村西蒲村一支参加龙舟赛的队伍专门设计制作的。他们后来又为大沥雅瑶制造了一条同样长的龙舟。虽然关家造龙舟业务已经遍及珠三角，甚至辐射到海外，近年来每年都能接到二三十条龙舟的订单，但是关氏父子对其前景并不感到乐观，将其定位为“夕阳产业”。究其原因主要有两点：

一是造龙舟辛苦沉闷且回报不高，年轻人宁愿去工厂打工也不愿意学造龙舟。现在关家造船厂内最年轻的师傅是出生于1973年的关永强兄弟俩，其他人已60岁左右，而关苏已经快70岁了。二是龙舟订单受政府政策的影响很大。2008年前后，由于奥运会和亚运会的影响，龙舟订单较多，2013年政府提倡节俭办节，关家造船厂的订单比2012年少了六成，生意非常冷清。

龙舟船身和龙舟头尾是分开制造的，关家造船厂只制造龙舟船身。关队在将龙舟厂交给儿子关苏打理之后，就退居幕后，在家雕刻龙头，供应关家造船厂。2007年，关队又收了一个徒弟，他就是同村的劳冠升，村人称其为九叔。劳冠升曾为造船工匠，后拜关队为师傅，跟着关队学做龙头，如今自己也开了一个小作坊，他制作的龙头主要供应关氏造船厂和三水其他的龙舟厂。

九叔制作的龙头
Dragon Heads Made by Uncle Nine

劳冠升师傅不足20平方米的作坊里摆满了大大小小的龙头，有的已经完工，有的还是半成品。龙舟头尾都是按客户要求定做的，各有特点，小龙头涂金漆无须，大龙头有涂金漆也有涂红漆，有黑须或白须，每个龙头都是张口见舌，舌面上有龙珠滚动，鹿角高翘，威风凛凛。据九叔介绍，制作龙头、龙尾要选质量上乘的檀木或樟木，直径需在

while in 2013 when the government was encouraging thrifty festivals, the Guans manufacturer witnessed a downturn in business with orders declined by 60% compared with those in 2012.

The making of the hull of a dragon boat is separate from that of the dragon head and tail. The Guans Dragon Boat Manufacturer only makes the hull of dragon boats. After handing the manufacturer over to his son Guan Su, Guan Dui took the back seat and began carving dragon heads at home to supply the manufacturer. In 2007, Guan Dui accepted another apprentice, Lao Guansheng, who lived in the same village and was called Uncle Nine by the villagers. He was once a boat builder and later learned making dragon heads from Guan Dui. Now, he is running a small workshop which mainly makes dragon heads for the Guans manufacturer and some other manufacturers in Sanshui District.

In master Lao Guansheng's small workshop of less than 20 square meters, there are dragon heads of all sizes, some finished and some half-finished. Dragon heads and tails are customized, having their own characteristics. Small dragon heads are painted with golden lacquer and without beards; big dragon heads with golden or red lacquer and with black or white beards. Each dragon's mouth is wide open. The tongue sticks out with a dragon ball on it. And the high and up dragon horns look majestic. According to Uncle Nine, the material of the dragon head and tail must be superior sandalwood or camphor wood and more than 30 centimeters in diameter. The high season of making dragon heads and tails is from the Spring Festival to the Dragon Boat Festival, during which Uncle Nine is very busy. Procedures of making dragon heads and tails are complicated, including selecting wood material, drawing, carving, forming, polishing, painting, decorating, etc. Given that, it takes at least one week to finish. Uncle Nine says it is very painstaking to make a dragon head because the maker has to imagine the shape of the dragon and to carve it according to customers' requirements. "Making dragon heads is laborious and boring while the earning is low, so young people are reluctant to do this work today. I guess I'm the only one still doing it in Sanshui." Uncle Nine can't help sighing when speaking of the inheritance of the skills of making dragon heads and tails. Although he has four children, none of them shows any interest in it. Now he is at the age of 80

九叔制作的龙头
Dragon Heads Made by Uncle Nine

and his health is getting worse, so it takes longer for him to carve a dragon head. Old as he is, Uncle Nine still sticks to his dragon boat dream. But it is quite hard to inherit the skills of making dragon boats.

Li Bao'an is also a renowned dragon boat builder in Foshan. He lives in Zhoubian Village of Sanshui District and has liked carpentry since he was young, though his elder generations were peasants. In 1959, Li Bao'an became an apprentice in Sanshui State-Owned Shipyard. He gradually mastered the skills of making ships there and then learned to make dragon boats from an old carpenter in the neighboring village. After mastering the skills, he was often invited by neighboring villages to make dragon boats. Around 2000, the newly retired Li Bao'an set up his own dragon boat manufacturer. His dragon boats became famous throughout the Pearl River Delta because of their good quality and fast speed. In 2017, the skill of building dragon boats in Zhoubian Village of Sanshui District was included into the sixth batch of intangible cultural heritages in Foshan. The Li family focuses on making five-people ones and also makes eleven-people, thirteen-people, fifty-people and even eighty-people ones to meet the needs of different customers. The basic procedures for building dragon boats of all sizes are identical. Since most procedures are finished manually, different boat builders make dragon boats with different unique features. Only when a dragon boat builder has abundant experience in the accuracy of the size of a dragon boat, the best radian of the hull, the buoyancy on the boat, the resistance to the boat and some other aspects can he build a light and fast dragon boat.

The Lis' dragon boats move quickly and steadily. Li Bao'an has revealed a few recipes for that. The first is customization. When someone places an order for

30厘米以上。每年的春节过后到端午节期间是造龙头、龙尾的旺季，这段时间九叔都非常忙。制作龙头、龙尾的工序繁杂，要找材料、画图、雕刻、成型、打磨、喷漆、装饰……最快也得一个星期才能出成品。九叔说，制作龙头很费心神，龙的形态完全靠想象，且龙头都是客户定做，必须按照客户要求雕刻出风格各异的龙头。谈起这门手艺的传承，九叔不免叹了一口气："做龙头费时又沉闷，赚的钱也少，现在的后生仔哪里愿意做，估计在三水只有我一个人在做了。"九叔虽有四个子女，但都对此无兴趣。现在九叔已经80岁了，身体也是每况愈下，雕刻龙头的速度因此变慢。耄耋之年的九叔还在坚守着自己的龙舟梦想，但龙舟制作技艺的传承之路却颇显崎岖。

李保安也是佛山出名的龙舟制造巧匠，是三水洲边村村民，父辈为农民，他少时喜爱做木工活。1959年，李保安进入三水国营船厂做学徒，逐渐掌握了造船的手艺，后来又向邻村一位老木匠学造龙舟。掌握了这门手艺后，李保安经常被邻近村落请去造龙舟。2000年前后，从三水造船厂退休的李保安自己开了一家龙舟制造厂。由于质量好、速度快，李家制造的龙舟誉满珠三角。2017年，佛山市三水洲边龙舟制作技艺进入佛山市第六批市级非遗名录。李家主要制造五人龙，也制作十一人龙、十三人龙、五十人龙甚至八十人龙，以满足更多客户的需求。无论哪一种规格的龙舟，基本工序是一致的，但由于龙舟大部分工序还是要靠人工，因此不同师傅制作的龙舟各有其独特之处。造龙舟师傅只有在龙舟尺寸的精确度、船身的最佳弧度、龙舟浮力、行船阻力等方面有丰富的经验，才能造出船身轻便、速度够快的龙舟。

李家龙舟划得又快又稳，李保安透露了其中的几个秘诀：其一是量身打造。有人来订船，李保安先要问清楚划这条船的扒丁的身形、体重，然后根据扒丁的总重来组装龙舟，形成不同的宽度和吃水深度，这种量身打造出来的“人船合一”的效果自然不错。其二是亲身测验。李保安的几个儿子在学习制作龙舟之初特意从顺德请了一支五人龙劲旅传授扒龙舟技巧，后来李家三兄弟也成了扒龙舟高手，他们将扒龙舟的心得转化为造船秘诀。比如龙舟在顺水、逆水、静水状态下，所受到的阻力各不相同，他们就将龙舟头尾弧度变小，直至趋向平直。其三是慢工出细活。“古话讲，‘求快做不出好东西’。我多花点时间，做好一点，人家自然会说好。”这是李保安经常对儿子们说的话。即使现在他很少亲自动手，但作为龙舟厂的技术监督，他还是经常提醒儿子们不能贪快，“慢工出细活”的古训不能忘。

龙舟参加比赛得了好名次，对方会送锦旗给李保安。龙船厂的一面墙上已经挂满了锦旗。其中一面锦旗上写着“三水李保安龙舟厂巧夺天工，香港南鹰龙舟会敬赠”，这是香港南鹰龙舟会赠送的。而最让李保安自豪的，是他曾打造九江龙舟队亚运会训练龙舟。

李保安有四个儿子，其中三个从事龙舟制造，大儿子李显能还在南海丹灶金沙下安白沙村独立开办了龙舟厂，主造五人龙。关于龙舟制造技艺的未来，李保安很乐观：“只要技术好，不愁没出路，不愁没人传承衣钵。”

a dragon boat, he will ask about the figures and weights of the paddlers and then assemble the boat in accordance with the total weight of the paddlers to form unique width and draught of the boat. This kind of customization, taking paddlers and the dragon boat into consideration, works well. The second is first-hand experience. At the beginning of learning to make dragon boats, Li Bao'an's sons specially invited a strong team of a five-people dragon boat racer from Shunde to impart skills of dragon boating. Afterwards, three of his sons have become excellent dragon boat racers and have applied what they have learnt in dragon boating to making dragon boats. For example, the resistance varies when a dragon boat is moving downstream, upstream or in still water, so they adjust the radian of the dragon head and tail to be nearly straight. The third is that soft fire makes sweet malt. "As an old saying goes, blindly seeking fast speed cannot make a good product. If we spend more time and do better, people will praise our work." This is what Li Bao'an often says to his sons. Even if he seldom makes dragon boats personally now, Li Bao'an, as the technical director of the manufacturer, still often reminds his sons not to blindly seek fast speed in the making and not to forget the old wisdom that the soft fire makes sweet malt.

Dragon boat racers will give a silk banner to thank Li Bao'an if they get a good result with Li's dragon boat in a race. Today, one wall of his manufacturer is covered with silk banners. One of them writes "Wonderful Skills of Li Bao'an Dragon Boat Manufacturer in Sanshui, by South Eagles Dragon Boat Association". What Li Bao'an is most proud of is that he once made the training dragon boats for Jiujiang Dragon Boat Team for the Asian Games.

Li Bao'an has four sons, three of whom are engaged in building dragon boats. His eldest son Li Xianneng has a dragon boat manufacturer of his own, mainly making five-people dragon boats, in Baisha Village of Jinshaxia'an of Nanhai District. "As long as we have superb skills, I'm not worried about the sales and the inheritance", Li Bao'an is optimistic about the future of dragon boat building skills.

FOSHAN

第三章 龙舟习俗 礼仪周到

Chapter 3 Dragon Boat Customs and Etiquettes

佛山扒龙舟习俗已经有上千年的历史，形成了一套完整的程序和神秘的礼仪，构成了佛山龙舟文化的核心。佛山龙舟习俗的程序与礼仪主要有起龙、采青、招景、探亲、迎龙、龙舟盛会、洗（喝）龙舟水、吃龙舟饭、散龙和藏龙等。采青的神秘、招景迎龙时浓浓的乡情、龙舟赛的激烈与惊险、吃龙舟饭的喜悦，展现出了佛山水乡别样的魅力。

Foshan dragon boat customs, with a history of over a thousand years, has formed a complete set of rituals and mysterious etiquettes, which constitute the core of Foshan dragon boat culture. The rituals and etiquettes of Foshan dragon boat customs mainly include lifting the dragon, collecting the greens, inviting and visiting sworn brothers, welcoming visiting dragons, enjoying the dragon boat gala, bathing in and drinking dragon boat water, having dragon boat meals, and separating and hiding the dragon. All these rituals show the unique charm of Foshan as a waterside city.

起龙
Lifting the Dragon Boat

3.1 Lifting the Dragon Boat

In Foshan, dragon boats are patron saints of each village. Any activity about the dragon boat is sacred and crucial. Therefore, as the beginning of a year's dragon boat activities, lifting the dragon boat, which means taking the dragon boat out of the river, is of vital importance.

The Foshan dragon boat activities are usually held around the Dragon Boat Festival (on the 5th day of the 5th lunar month), so lift the dragon boat mostly happens in the middle and late period of the fourth lunar month. But sometimes this ritual is carried out in early spring mainly for two reasons. One is to dry the dragon boat completely because it has been buried in the water for a long time and soaked up a lot of water. The other is to exercise early to strive for good results in the dragon boat races that year. If the dragon boat just participates in the cruises instead of the races, it can be lifted only three to five days in advance. The day of lifting the dragon boat must be carefully selected. Villagers will refer to the almanac or the perpetual calendar to choose a lucky day. At the same time, the weather must be good, and it is best to be a public holiday so that everyone can come to help. Before lifting the dragon boat, villagers will go to the village temple or public activity room to take out the dragon head, dragon tail, the gongs and drums, then village elders will hold a simple worship ceremony. In the old days, people paid more particular attention to the ritual of lifting the dragon boat. For example, villagers would get up early to pray for a smooth day, and those who participated in the ritual would bow to each other with hands folded in front to show courtesy. At the same time, the villagers should also send "mud cakes" to the brawny men who were responsible for lifting the dragon boat, wishing them "good luck". Lifting the dragon boat is a strenuous task that

第一节　起龙

在佛山水乡，龙舟就是一个村落的保护神，关于龙舟的任何一次活动都是神圣的，也是至关重要的。起龙舟是一年龙舟活动的开端，其重要性不言而喻。

佛山龙舟活动大都在端午节前后举办，因此起龙舟大多是在4月中下旬进行。但也有一些龙舟起得比较早，在早春时节就起龙舟，一则因为龙舟埋藏在水中，船身蕴藏的水分较多，早点起上来便于晾干；二则“早起早锻炼”，以争取在当年的龙舟赛中获得好成绩。如果当年不参加比赛，只参加游龙，则提前三五天起龙舟即可。起龙舟的日子一定要精心挑选，人们会看皇历或万年历选一个好日子，同时那天要天气好，且最好是公众假期，方便大家来帮忙。在起龙舟前，大家要去存放龙头、龙尾和龙船锣鼓的社庙或公共活动室，将龙头、龙尾和龙船锣鼓取出来，由村中长老主持举行一个简单的拜神仪式。旧时起龙舟有更多讲究，起龙舟那天村民都要早早起床，祈求起龙时顺顺利利，参加起龙舟的人都要互相作揖，以表礼节。同时，村民还要给参与起龙舟的壮汉们发泥饼，预祝有个“好意头”。吉时一到，穿着短裤的人们就跳进水中，大家或拉或抬，合力将龙舟起出河面。现在有些村落已经不用人力起龙舟，而是使用吊机来吊。起龙舟是一个力气活，需要青壮年参与。起龙舟的时间视淤泥的多少与藏龙的深度而定，最少都要一个小时。在整个起龙舟的过程中，人们一直敲锣打鼓和放鞭炮。

龙舟起上来后，人们情绪高涨，就会用各种方式来庆祝一番，互相泼水、扔泥巴是最为常见的。水中的人们用勺子或小盆舀起一盆盆水，互相泼洒嬉戏；岸上的人们说了什么笑话，惹得水中的人向他们拼命泼水，岸上的人就用土块当武器回击，一时之间，你来我往，嬉笑声、尖叫声、锣鼓声、鞭炮声交织在一起，好一幅活泼喧闹的水乡风情画。闹毕笑毕，人们就把龙舟扒到旁边，由专人清洗干净。现在有些村落不太注重传统，起龙舟时没有任何仪式，静悄悄地起龙舟，没什么龙舟活动的热闹气氛。

龙舟被清理干净后，就会被抬上涌边树荫下搭好的木架上或者抬至村中会所，以晾干水分，龙舟上还要搭纤维布，因为坤甸木最怕风吹日晒。经历了上一年龙舟活动中数日的访阿契、激烈的竞渡、惊险的龙舟出海，龙舟难免有磕磕碰碰，因此都需要对龙舟进行仔细的检查和整修。首先查看龙舟的龙底、龙骨、大旁、龙筋等主体结构有没有残缺或破损，并根据残破程度进行修补或更换。简单的维护，可以打电话给船厂的人来处理，如果主体结构出了问题就须将船运到船厂去修理。

龙舟经过检查没有什么大碍，就开始紧龙筋。龙筋的松紧度要把握好，这个工序最能体现师傅的功力。龙筋扎得太松，龙舟两头就不会翘起来，难以形成龙的形状，下水后船身中部还容易拱起来，左右摇晃不定，速度当然也快不起来；龙筋扎得太紧，龙舟头

requires the joint efforts of a lot of people. At the auspicious moment, brawny men in shorts, jumping into the river, pull or drag together to lift the dragon boat out of the river. Now some villages use cranes instead of manpower to hoist the dragon boat. The length of time it takes to lift the dragon boat depends on the amount of silt and the depth of the buried dragon boat, but is at least one hour. In the whole process of lifting the dragon boat, the sounds of gongs and drums as well as firecrackers should never stop.

南海九江起龙舟
Lifting the Dragon in Jiujiang, Nanhai

With the dragon boat lifted, villagers are in high spirits, celebrating it in various ways, the most common of which is to splash water or throw mud at each other. People in the river scoop up water to splash and play with each other. When people standing on the banks say something funny, those in the river will splash water at them while the former fight back with mud. They play with each other merrily for some time. Laughter, screams, and sounds of drums, gongs, and firecrackers are intertwined to create a lively and bustling scene of a water village. After having fun, they row the dragon boat to the side to have it cleaned. Now, some villages have ignored this ritual, so there is no ceremony to lift the dragon boat.

After being cleaned, the dragon boat is carried to the wooden stand set up in the shade of the tree along the river or placed in the village clubhouse to dry. The dragon boat also needs to be covered with a fiber cloth, because it is made of Pontianak wood that can hardly stand the wind and the sun. Besides, after several intense and thrilling activities of visiting sworn brothers, racing, and cruising in the previous year the dragon boat is inevitably damaged by bumps, so it needs to be carefully inspected and repaired. First the main structure of the dragon boat is checked, including the bottom board, the keel, the sideboards and the tendons. Then the worn or torn parts are repaired or replaced according to the degree of damage. If it needs only simple maintenance, boatyard workers can come to fix it; but if there is any problem with the main structure, it has to be sent back to the boatyard to be repaired.

If there are no serious problems with the dragon boat, the villagers will continue to tighten the dragon tendons. It is vital to adjust the tendons to the most suitable tightness, and this process can best represent the craftsman's skills. On the one hand, if the dragon tendons are too loose, the boat will not hold its head high and cock its tail up, making it unlike a dragon; besides, after the boat enters the water, the middle of the hull is easy to arch, and the boat will sway left and right, thus slowing down the speed. On the other hand, if the tendons are too tight, the head and tail of the boat will be so high that the boat sways, too. After the dragon tendons are properly tightened, the craftsman needs to jump up and down on the bow and stern to test the flexibility of the hull.

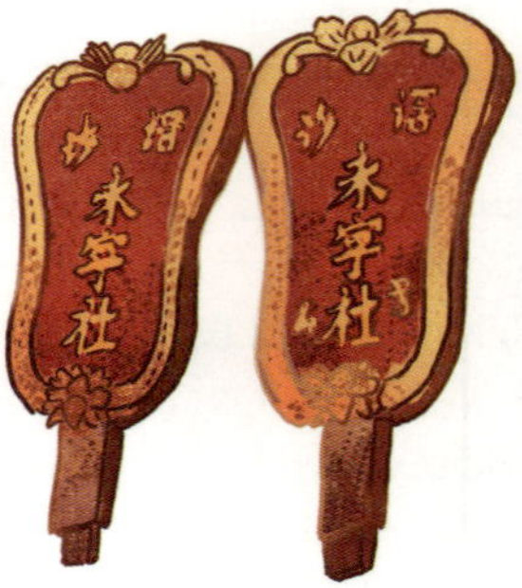

龙牌
Dragon Cards

The next step is to polish the dragon boat with oil. In the past, villagers used lard or fat pork. Now wood oil is a better choice. The reason for oiling the dragon is to protect the Pontianak wood from cracking and to make the dragon boat smoother and swifter. After a year's preservation, the dragon head and tail are covered with a layer of dust, so they need to be cleaned or even repainted.

The repair and renovation is followed by decoration of the dragon boat. As mentioned above, the decorations of the racing and cruising dragon boats are quite different. A racing dragon boat is equipped only with its dragon card and the dragon drum, while a cruising dragon boat is equipped with its dragon card,

尾上翘太高，龙舟入水后也会左右摇晃。龙筋扎好后，师傅还要站在船头船尾跳几下，试试船体的柔韧度。

接下来就是给龙舟刷油，以前都是刷猪油或者用几块肥猪肉擦船，现在一般是刷木油。之所以要刷油，一是为了保护龙舟的制造材料坤甸木不开裂，二是刷了油的龙舟更滑溜，赛龙时速度会更快。龙头、龙尾经过了一年的存放也蒙上了不少灰尘，要擦洗干净，有些还要重新上漆。龙舟整修好后，就要进行装饰。赛龙和彩龙的装饰大有不同，上文讲过赛龙只配备必需的龙牌、龙船鼓，彩龙则配备有龙牌、罗伞、锣鼓、旗帜和其他装饰。

顺德龙舟起上来后还有一个拜神、请神的仪式，也就是请村中社庙神灵的“行宫”到龙舟上充当龙舟保护神。负责神楼的扒丁要先上香祭拜社庙中的神灵，拜完神之后持着点燃的香和香油，送到龙舟上，然后再虔诚地将供奉在社庙中的神灵“行宫”请到龙舟的神楼中，并在船头和船尾贴上符咒，祈求龙舟活动顺风顺水、大吉大利。

装饰好的龙舟，一般还要举行一个进水仪式，旧龙舟和新龙舟的进水仪式是不同的。旧龙舟进水仪式在从前比较复杂，先要选定一个吉日吉时，由召集人带领村中或族中参与龙舟活动的青壮年，来到宗祠、社庙或江河边，烧香烛，燃放鞭炮，并由德高望重的老者做一番祈祷，祈求龙舟在比赛中获胜，祝福周边一带人丁兴旺、风调雨顺。祷毕，众人再合力抬起龙舟慢慢放入水中，扒丁上船扒龙舟，绕行村落游龙。现在很多村落的旧龙舟已经不再举行进水仪式，或者只是简单祭拜一下。

新龙舟制作好后，人们会挑选一个黄道吉日迎接新龙舟回家，举行新龙舟进水仪式。新龙舟到达村子附近时，旧龙舟和阿契就要去迎接，然后所有龙舟的扒丁要拿着自己的龙头、龙尾、龙牌到社庙中燃烛烧香祭拜。众人祭拜完后，就把龙头、龙尾安装到龙舟上，再为新龙舟点睛。龙舟点睛的礼仪很隆重，人们要先将预备好的符咒贴在船头、船尾和锣鼓上面，上一炷香（祈求第一名），摆上鸡（不能用四个齿鸡冠的鸡，人们认为“四”字不吉利）、烧肉、水果（不能用苹果，怕成绩平平；喜欢用雪梨，意为“伶伶俐俐”）、葱（取“向前冲”之意）；然后请南无佬（主持拜神活动的民间道士）穿上巫衣，手持木剑，口诵祝词，燃烧符咒，用朱砂为龙头点睛，用黄皮叶蘸水由船头洒到船尾，用剑拍击船尾，祈

龙舟点睛
Dotting the Dragon Eyes

special umbrellas, gongs and drums,flags as well as other decorations.

In Shunde District of Foshan City, after the dragon boat is lifted, there is an additional ritual to worship and invite the gods, that is, to invite the travelling statue of the god in the village to the dragon boat as its patron saint. The paddler who is in charge of the small shrine in the boat cabin must first light incenses and worship the god in the village temple, carry the lit incenses and the oil to the dragon boat, and then devoutly invite the god's travelling statue to the small shrine in the boat. The final step is to put the spells on the bow and stern, praying for a smooth and successful dragon boat festival.

After the dragon boat has been decorated, there is a water entry ceremony, which differs for an old dragon boat and a new one. That for an old one was much more complicated. First, an auspicious hour on an auspicious day should be chosen, at which time the convener led the strong young men, who participated in the dragon boat activities, to gather in the ancestral hall or village temple or by the riverside. Then they burnt incenses and set off firecrackers; the highly respected elders prayed for their victory in the dragon boat races and for prosperity and good weather for the crops in the neighborhoods. After the ceremony, the crowd carried the dragon boat together and slowly sent it into the creek. The paddlers boarded it and rowed it around the village. But nowadays, people in many villages no longer hold a water entry ceremony for the old dragon boats, instead they just worship the gods simply.

When a new dragon boat is made, the villagers will also pick an auspicious day to welcome it home and hold a water entry ceremony. Before the new dragon boat reaches the village, the old ones and the sworn brothers need to greet it. Then all the paddlers should take the dragon head, the dragon tail, and the dragon card to the village temple to burn incenses and worship. After everyone has finished worshiping, the dragon head and the dragon tail are reassembled on the boat. Then it is time to dot the dragon eyes, which is a grand ritual. Villagers should first put the prepared spells on the bow, stern, and gongs and drums. They then offer one burning joss stick (praying to be No. 1), and put on the rooster (not using four-tooth comb roosters as "four" is an unlucky number in Chinese), roast pork, fruit (using pears instead of apples) and scallions (symbolizing striving forward). The folk priest, in his priest frock and with a wooden sword, will recite blessing words, burn spells, and then dot the eyes of the dragon with cinnabar. He would also use Chinese wampee leaves to dip water and sprinkle it from the bow to the stern, and use the sword to pat the stern, praying for good racing results, good weather throughout the year and the prosperity for the village. The new dragon boat that has its eyes dotted will be dragged into the creek and start cruising around the village. Generally, the first to row the new dragon boat are the children, followed by the elderly who like dragon boats, and the last are young and middle-aged men. Some villages will specially build a dragon gate for the boat to cross. The cruise is to show the new home to the dragon boat so that it can soon settle down in the village as the patron saint. In the past, people on the banks would throw carps into the water when the new dragon boat crossed the dragon gate, which is believed to be an auspicious omen.

Gemei Village, Sanshui District, Foshan, is located by the Xijiang River. Its villagers are passionate about dragon boats. All men, young and old, like dragon boating. Their dragon boat cruise is different from that of other places. According to the elderly in the village, on the eve of the dragon boat race every year, the dragon head and the dragon tail are taken off the dragon boat and carried by men to tour around the village for several rounds. It is said that this ritual can bring good luck to the village.

求比赛取得好成绩，全年风调雨顺、财源广进。点睛后的新龙舟被拖入水中，开始在村中河涌里巡游，称为“游地头”。一般最先扒新龙舟“游地头”的是村中的小孩，接着是村中喜欢龙舟的老人，最后是青壮年，有些村落还专门搭建了龙门供龙舟穿越。大家兴致勃勃地扒着新龙舟巡游整条村，让新龙舟认识自己的家，并在此安家，保佑村庄风调雨顺、旺丁旺财。以前新龙舟穿越龙门的时候，岸上的人还会扔鲤鱼，寓意“鱼跃龙门”。

三水西南阁美村位于西江边，村人对龙舟有着特殊的感情，只要是男丁，无论老少，都喜欢划龙舟。他们的游龙与其他地方又有不同，据村中老人讲，每年龙舟比赛的前夕，村里人都会把龙舟的龙头和龙尾拆下来，让村里面的男丁抬着围绕着村子转数圈，据说这样可以为村人带来好运气。

第二节　采青

据说龙舟沉睡了一年，头昏脑涨没有精神，食了青才会有精神，赛龙才会生猛。因此龙舟采青是传统龙舟活动中的一个重要环节，寓意一年龙舟节的正式开始。

“十里不同风，百里不同俗”，佛山各地采青的时间和形式也各有特点。南海九江龙舟采青的时间在龙舟活动前某天的凌晨（午夜十二点至凌晨四五点），新龙采青的日子通常比较早，往往在“入伙”（新龙进水仪式）后就进行。九江人之所以要选择凌晨出

龙船采青（九江文化站）
Dragon Boats Collecting the Greens (Jiujiang Township Cultural Station)

3.2 Collecting the Greens

It is said that the dragon boat is dizzy because of a year's sleep. It can only become energetic in races after eating the greens. Therefore, collecting the greens is one of the most important parts in traditional dragon boat activities, which signifies the formal beginning of the Dragon Boat Festival.

As the old saying goes, customs vary from place to place. The time and form of collecting the greens around Foshan have their own characteristics. Collecting the greens in Jiujiang, Nanhai District, usually starts in the early morning (from midnight to 4 or 5 a.m.) of someday before the dragon boat activities. If the dragon boat is new, it is usually carried out just after the water entry ceremony. People in Jiujiang prefer to collect the greens before dawn to avoid being seen by pregnant women, women who gave birth less than 100 days ago and people from other villages,following an old tradition. Instead of playing the drums and gongs on the way to the collecting site, people row the decorated dragon boat quietly. The location for the activity must be a place that can offer happiness, prosperity, longevity and fortune. Generally, the site is fixed. On arrival, people burn incenses, candles and dragon clothes made of paper and the highly respected person will collect the greens, which can be branches of grapefruit, longan, pomegranates and pines. The leaves are then fed into the dragon's mouth. For a new dragon boat, the above four kinds of greens can be picked but for the old ones, only the first three are chosen. After collecting the greens, people will row the dragon boat in high spirits back and forth in the creek with the boisterous sound of firecrackers, drums and gongs. Back in the village, the paddlers hurry to the teahouse for morning tea (a kind of Cantonese breakfast) and discuss the coming activities.

采青
Collecting the Greens

There were a lot of taboos about collecting the greens in Jiujiang. Many people had no chance to enjoy this activity, including women, people from other villages, those men whose wives were pregnant or had just given birth, or the men whose families were involved in unlucky or bad things. Additionally, men who had happy events in their homes in the same month could not participate in collecting the greens, because people there believed that the joyful event and collecting the greens would oppose each other and one of them would suffer. Most of these taboos have been dropped due to the advances in science, but outsiders are still prohibited from seeing this activity, which obviously shows its mystery and importance in Jiujiang.

Collecting the greens in Daliang, Shunde District takes place in the daytime. People collect a handful of grass from the creek near the village and feed it into the dragon's mouth. Before the 1980s and 1990s, water courses in Daliang were clear so that the greens could be collected near the Qingyun Tower in Shunfeng Mountain. However, because many rivers and creeks are now blocked up, the ceremony has to be simplified so that the greens are collected in the creek near the village, but the dragon head should point to the direction of the Qingyun Tower.

发采青，是因为传统的禁忌，要避免被孕妇、生子未过百日的产妇和外村人看到。前往采青点的途中一般不会敲锣打鼓，大家划着装饰好的龙舟静静前往。采青地点的选择也是有讲究的，要找能聚福禄寿财的地方，一般一艘龙舟会多年固定去同一地点采青。到达采青点后，先要烧香烛、龙衣等，然后由德高望重者去采青。所采之青可以是柚子枝、龙眼枝、石榴枝、松柏枝等，当年新造的龙舟以上四种都可采，旧龙舟不采松柏，采来的青塞在龙嘴中。采好青后就烧鞭炮，鼓锣齐响，食了青的龙舟精神勃发，在河涌中扒几个来回后才往回扒。回到村中，扒丁们就赶去茶楼喝个早茶，商量接下来的龙舟活动事宜。

九江龙舟采青以前有很多禁忌，如女人不能看采青，外人不能看采青，妻子怀孕或妻子刚生孩子的男人不能去采青，家中发生了不吉利的事或丑事的男人不能参与采青，当月内家中有喜事的男人也不能去采青，因为喜事会与采青相冲，以致其中之一受损。现在科学昌明，已经没有那么多的禁忌了，但是外人不能看采青的传统还是保留了下来，足见九江龙舟采青的神秘性和重要性。

顺德大良龙舟采青安排在白天进行，就在村庄附近河涌边的水草丛中摘一把青草喂进龙嘴中。二十世纪八九十年代之前，大良河道畅通，采青仪式要到顺峰山的青云塔附近进行，但现在很多河涌淤积堵塞，采青仪式不得不简化，一般在村居附近的河涌进行，但龙头还是要对着青云塔的方向。

每年端午节前夕，盐步人会选择吉日起龙。在焚烧龙衣纸马，燃放香烛鞭炮，举行一个简单的祭龙仪式后，盐步的青壮年跳入龙床中，合力将老龙舟起出来，清洗干净，然后给龙舟装上龙头、龙尾、龙牌等装饰，再扒到龙涌河采青（俗称“进水”）。以前龙涌河两岸都是水稻田，起了龙舟后，就可以在附近的稻田采一把青青的禾苗，寓意风调雨顺、五谷丰登。由于盐步城市化的发展，现在龙涌河两岸已经没有稻田，只能在河涌边采一把绿意盎然的青草。

高明墨编村也是在白天采青，所采之青为稻穗，寓意该村今年将会风调雨顺、五谷丰登。

佛山龙舟所采之青都要喂进龙嘴中或绑在龙角上，保存到藏龙前的最后一刻才会被取下，放在藏龙的水域边或藏龙头、龙尾的社庙旁。

Before the Dragon Boat Festival every year, the Yanbu people will choose an auspicious day to lift the dragon. After a simple dragon worshiping ceremony by burning dragon garments, paper horses and incenses, and setting off firecrackers, the young and middle-aged people of Yanbu jump into the dragon bed to lift the old dragon boat out of water. They then clean it and decorate it with the dragon head, tail and card and row it the Longchong Creek to collect the greens (commonly known as "entering water"). In the past, there were paddies on both sides of the creek, so after lifting the dragon boat, they could collect a bunch of grain seedlings in the surroundings to wish for nice weather and a bumper harvest. With the urbanization of Yanbu, those fields have already disappeared so that they can only pick a handful of grass by the creek instead.

Mobian Village in Gaoming District also collects the greens in the daytime. What people collect are ears of rice, meaning favorable weather for the crops and a bumper harvest in the year.

People put the greens collected by the dragon boat into the dragon's mouth or tie them to the horns and keep them there until the moment before the dragon boat is stored. After the event, the greens are kept by the creek where the dragon boat lies or the village temple that holds the dragon head and tail.

3.3 Inviting Sworn Brothers and Welcoming Dragon Boats

In Foshan, dragon boat activities are often not limited to people from one clan or village. Neighboring clans, villages and sworn brothers are also invited by notices and invitation cards to take part in the activities. This process is known as "Inviting Sworn Brothers and Welcoming the Dragon Boats". The dragon boat songs and dragon boat letters, as two important tools in the invitations, play an important role in conveying messages during the annual dragon boat activities.

The Dragon Boat Songs

The dragon boat song is a specific ballad for dragon boat racing and may have different names in different areas. Its form is relatively free, with a combination of three, five or seven Chinese characters in an intermixed way. Most dragon boat songs follow the rhythm and rhyme of Chinese classical poetry, and usually the rhythm is repeated in the whole song. In addition, some characteristics of the local folk songs are included, making them very catchy. The origin of composing dragon boat songs remains unknown but it's said that it was already quite popular in the Ming and Qing dynasties. At that time, local literati were invited to compose songs which would introduce the dragon boat racing from several aspects, such as the time, site, rules and schedules, and prizes for different rankings. The length of the songs might vary from dozens to hundreds of Chinese characters. Later on, the dragon boat songs serve as an overall introduction to the racing, and people add more information into it, including the local economy, culture, folk customs and development, making the whole song as long as over one thousand Chinese characters. Such dragon boat songs

第三节　招景迎龙

佛山龙舟活动参加者众，除了所属的宗族或村落，还要邀请相邻宗族、村落、兄弟契友等来参加活动，因此需要发出通知和邀请，欢迎他们的到来，这就是招景迎龙。龙舟歌标、龙船帖是招景的重要工具，在一年一度的龙舟活动中起着传递信息的重要作用。

龙舟歌标

又称歌标、标歌或龙船引，有“高歌夺标”的意思，是举办龙舟赛时所使用的特定歌谣。其形式比较自由，多用三、五、七字作为间隔组合，沿袭古典诗词的声律和押韵，大多数都是一韵到底，也带有一些当地民谣的特点，读起来朗朗上口。龙舟歌标起于何时难以考究，据说明清时期已经非常流行，当时多请当地文人撰写，其内容包括了赛龙时间、地点、规程、奖品、奖励名次等要素，短的数十字，长的可达数百字。后来有人提炼“赛龙起引”作为龙舟赛的总体介绍，并在歌标中加入当地的经济文化、民俗风情、发展情况等内容，一篇可达上千字。这样的龙舟歌标张贴到各地，具有通知、公告和发动的意义，起到了发送“英雄帖”的作用。

一般在赛龙前的半个月，组织者就会请人创作歌标，并用大红纸书写好后张贴至各村。人们根据龙舟歌标就了解到了龙舟赛的基本内容，做好各种事项的准备，提前邀请亲戚朋友来看龙舟赛。如果是公开邀请赛的歌标，还跨村跨县张贴到各地。歌标所到之处，必然会引起阵阵轰动，参加赛事的摩拳擦掌，看赛事的议论纷纷，又有一番热闹可看了。龙舟赛时，百舸争流，人潮如织，气氛热烈，与龙舟歌标有着莫大的关系。

歌标包含的信息丰富，读起来朗朗上口，雅俗共赏，在佛山风行了数百年。可惜随着白话文的出现和赛事的变革，歌标这一传统文艺形式逐渐式微，尤其是在信息传递方式多样化的今天，已经难觅歌标的踪影，佛山会写龙舟歌标的人也已经屈指可数了。在三水白坭，有几位会写作龙舟歌标的老人，最著名的就是被称为“歌标王”的徐国林。“迎得中华崛起，亚洲正茂风华。运交华盖是谁家？我粤平添身价。镇域欢歌竞渡，龙门逐鹿并扒！舟冲水溅浪飞花，赛到休标方罢。”这是徐国林为白坭镇2010年“迎亚运”龙舟竞渡大赛创作的歌标，以西江月词牌创作藏头诗作为赛龙起引，每一句词开头的第一个字合起来就是“迎亚运我镇龙舟赛”，对龙舟赛做了总体介绍；然后就是龙舟歌标正文，内容包括白坭镇的发展情况、工农业概况、民生、龙舟文化、赛

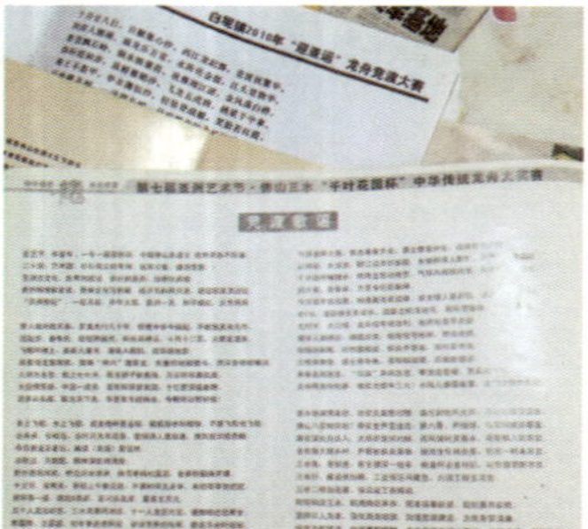

龙舟歌标
Dragon Boat Songs

are posted in various places to notify and mobilize potential participants, just like "Hero Invitation Cards" in China's traditional martial arts.

Usually half a month before the dragon boat racing, a dragon boat song will be composed, then written on pieces of bright red paper and posted in different villages. With the song, people can know the basic information about the racing, get prepared for various activities, and invite friends and relatives to watch the racing in advance. If the song is for an open invitational racing, then it will even be posted in other towns and counties. The song causes a sensation wherever it goes, with participants being eager for the racing, and the audience talking about this grand occasion. It is largely because of the dragon boat songs that we can see hundreds of boats competing for the championship in the dragon boat racing held on the exact day, creating a euphoric atmosphere and attracting large numbers of audiences.

Being informative and catchy, dragon boat songs have prevailed in Foshan for hundreds of years among people with different aesthetic tastes. It is a pity that this traditional form of art has gradually become less popular as a result of the advent of writings in the vernacular and changes in the dragon boat racing. Especially, with diversified messaging channels today, it is difficult to find such songs, and only a mere handful of people in Foshan know how to write them. For example, in the town of Baini in Sanshui District, there are several such elders, the most famous of whom is Xu Guolin, also known as "The King of Dragon Boat Songs". To welcome the Asian Games held in Guangzhou in 2010, and the dragon boat racing in particular, Xu composed a dragon boat song for Baini Town in a traditional poetry structure. The song, in the form of an acrostic poem, gives an overall introduction to the racing at the beginning with the first Chinese character of each line together forming a sentence, meaning "To Welcome the Dragon Boat Racing in Our Town in Celebration of the Asian Games". Then there is the main body of the song, which covers several aspects of the Baini Town, such as the development, overview of industry and agriculture, people's livelihood and the dragon boat culture there, as well as detailed information about the racing such as rules, schedules and prizes.

Dragon Boat Letters

In the past, limited information exchange channels led to an inconvenience in communication with others, so dragon boat letters were used to spread news about the dragon boat activities to be held in their own villages or clans. Such letters are a common cultural symbol of Foshan dragon boat activities. They are simple in form, written on a piece of red paper to convey the information. In the past, they were written with writing brushes. When invitation letters with different styles of Chinese calligraphy were posted all over the wall, it was quite a sensational scene. Nowadays many of them are printed instead of handwritten. As a result, though the content and function remain the same, they are less exciting.

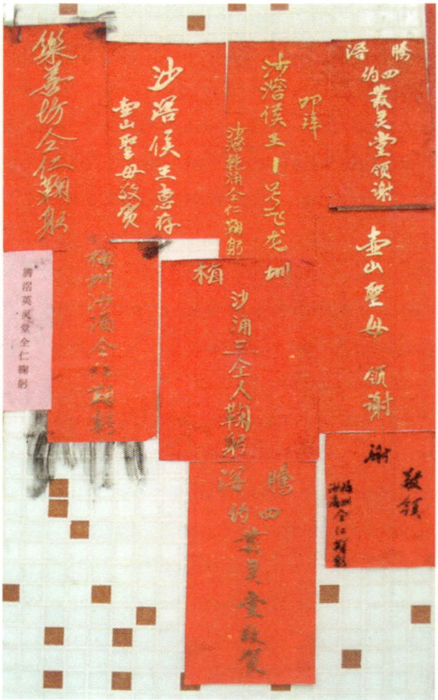

龙船帖
Dragon Boat Letters

According to different contents and purposes, dragon boat letters can be divided into two types, namely the invitation cards and the visiting cards (or thanks cards). By sending out invitation cards, the organizer invites relatives, sworn brothers and other dragon boat teams from neighboring villages to come to participate in the dragon boat activities and have dragon boat meals. The words in an invitation card may go like "we cordially invite ... (name of a dragon boat team) from your village to grace the Dragon Boat Festival activities to

事规程、奖金等，将龙舟赛事的具体细节交代得非常清楚。

龙船帖

旧时信息交流方式单一，通信不方便，人们为了传递自己村落或宗族的龙舟活动信息，就需要用到龙船帖，它是佛山水乡龙舟活动中常见的一种文化符号。龙船帖形式简单，就是在一张红纸上写上一排字，表明自己的意思即可。以前龙船帖都是以毛笔手写而成，各种不同字体的龙船帖贴满墙壁，显得热闹而有个性，而今不少龙舟使用打印的龙船帖，内容与作用虽无差别，但其中的韵味却有很大不同。

按不同的内容与作用，龙船帖分为两种，即龙船请帖、龙船拜帖或谢帖。龙船请帖，是由主办方向友好邻村发出的邀请帖，请亲戚、契友和龙舟队伍前来参加龙舟盛会、吃龙舟饭等，上书如“请贵村××龙舟五月初五驾临×村，游龙增光，敬备茶水恭候”或“……敬备薄酌恭候”。龙船请帖体现了村落之间的礼尚往来，避免了不请自来的尴尬。每年龙舟节前夕，招景村落的龙船会就会派村中父老，带上龙船请帖前往兄弟或契友村落，向对方发出邀请，让对方做好准备。旧时交通不发达，去比较远的村落送龙船请帖需要划数小时船，送上帖后，还需住上一宿，次日才能返回，但人们仍乐此不疲。现在通信发达，虽通过电话、短信、微信、传真等都可以非常快速方便地通知对方，但人们还是坚持采用这种传统的方式，让人感受到了传统的力量和兄弟契友之间的深情。送完龙船请帖，龙舟活动算是拉开了序幕。兄弟村落欣然接受，决定参加，称为“应景”。龙船景当日应景村落如约赴会，如果只表演技巧，展示装饰，称为“趁景”；如果赛龙排名次，就称“斗标”。

龙船拜帖或谢帖是龙船拜访别人时所用的名帖，主要是向被拜访者表明来访者的身份，让对方先了解自己，请求给予接待与帮助，同时表达对主人的谢意，在龙舟节前夕或者当日送出。简单的龙船拜帖就是在一张红纸上印上“××龙船会叩谢”“××龙船会领谢”，复杂点的会在上面印上龙、蝙蝠等吉祥图案。

龙船帖
A Dragon Boat Letter

龙船帖送到后，主办方会将龙船帖贴在村中祠堂、会所、村委会等公共场所的墙上或者公告栏上。之所以要贴在公共场所，一是为了展示本村的经济实力和人缘，因为来访的龙舟越多，就表明该村的经济实力越强，人缘越好，村子越有威望，村里的人也会觉得很有面子；二是为了财务公开，有龙舟来拜访就需要接待，要送水、水果、高标，请吃龙船饭等，来拜访的龙舟越多，所需花费也就越高，而龙舟活动的经费都是通过各种途径募集来的公有经费，龙船帖就是一个极好的支出证明。

be held on the fifth day of the fifth lunar month with your presence. We have prepared tea and food/simple meals". Sending out invitation cards is a kind of courtesy exchange, and it can help avoid the embarrassing situation of having uninvited dragon boats. Every year, before celebrating the Dragon Boat Festival, the dragon boat club from the host village has the elders in the village send invitation cards to sworn brother villages, so the latter can make preparations in advance. It took several hours to paddle to a distant village since transportation was underdeveloped in the old days. After extending the invitation cards, people needed to stay for one night before returning. Despite the inconvenience, people enjoyed this tradition and never got tired of it. Today communication is quick and convenient by phone, text message, WeChat, fax, etc. However, people still cling to the tradition of sending invitation cards in person, which reflects the power of traditions and the brotherhood and friendship between villages. The dragon boat racing begins after invitation cards are sent out. The invited dragon boats can choose only to show their rowing skills and decorations or to take part in the racing to win prizes.

Visiting cards or thanks cards are presented prior to or on the visiting day. With visiting cards, the guests extend their gratitude and introduce themselves, so the organizer can know them in advance and get ready to welcome them. A simple form of the visiting card is just a piece of red paper with "Sincere thanks from... (name of a dragon boat club)" on it, and more complicated ones may have auspicious patterns such as dragons and bats.

The visiting cards received are posted on the wall or bulletin boards in public places such as ancestral halls, clubs and village committees. There are two reasons to do so. The first is to showcase economic strength and popularity. Many dragon boats coming as guests mean that the host village is rich, popular and prestigious, and villagers are also proud of that. The second is to ensure financial transparency. To receive the visiting dragon boats requires drinks, fruits, *Gaobiao*, dragon boat meals and so on. The more dragon boats come, the higher the expenditure is. As the dragon boat activities are financed by public funds collected through various channels, the visiting cards are excellent certificates of expenditures.

Visiting Relatives and Welcoming Dragon Boats

What follows is the ceremony called "Visiting Relatives". The newly renovated dragon boats, decorated with the dragon head and tail, special umbrellas and colorful flags, come to visit relatives amid sounds of drums and gongs. When the guest dragon boat is about to enter the creek of the host village, the host village sends a dragon boat to welcome the guest, amid sounds of drums, gongs and firecrackers. When the two dragon boats meet each other, people on the boats must stop drumming and whoop several times to greet each other. When the guest dragon boat has entered the creek of the host village, amid loud sounds of drums, gongs and firecrackers, the person in charge of the host dragon boat club leads the villagers to the riverside to greet the guests with the fist-and-palm salute. Villagers warmly invite the guests ashore to enjoy dragon boat cakes, have small talks and dragon boat meals. In some villages, dragon gates are built specially over the creek. And the joyous atmosphere reaches its climax when dragon boats pass through the gate to the sound of the applause, drums, gongs, fire crackers as well as gun salutes. The guest dragon boats are not in a hurry to get ashore, but express their appreciation and salute to the hosts with cheerful drumbeats and gong sounds and loud shouts. In addition, the guests have to paddle the boats back and forth for three rounds between the river mouth and the village temple or the pond, before laying their paddles down and getting ashore. The guests first stick the visiting cards on the wall of the ancestral hall or village temple of the host village before eating the dragon boat meals.

探亲、迎龙

贴出龙舟歌标和发出龙船帖后，龙舟就要探亲了。整修一新的龙舟装上龙头、龙尾、罗伞和幡旗，一路敲锣打鼓，踏上了探亲之旅。当探亲的龙舟即将进入主家河涌时，主家村落会派龙舟出来迎接，敲锣打鼓放鞭炮以示欢迎，两龙相遇时必须停鼓呐喊数声。探亲龙舟进入主家河涌后，主家龙船会负责人带领村民来到河边，向前来的龙舟拱手欢迎，同时锣鼓喧天、鞭炮齐鸣，热情邀请对方上岸吃饼叙旧、吃龙船饭。有些村落还在河涌上专门搭建了供龙舟穿越的龙门，所有龙舟高高兴兴地划过龙门，岸上的人喝彩鼓掌，敲锣打鼓，燃放鞭炮和礼炮，将欢乐的气氛推向高潮。此时前来的龙舟并不急着上岸，而是用欢快的锣鼓节奏和大声呐喊向主办方表示感谢，同时龙舟还要在涌口至社庙或涌口至池塘之间的水域来回三次，才落扒上岸，先往主家村落的祠堂或社庙前贴上龙船帖，再吃龙舟饭。

第四节　龙舟盛会

龙舟盛会也称为“龙船盛会”。佛山龙舟盛会有两种形式，即赛龙斗标和彩龙竞艳，赛龙主要在于比速度的快慢，俗称斗标或竞渡；竞艳主要看龙舟的外观装饰和扒龙舟的技巧，又称为“趁景”。龙舟盛会是一年一度的龙舟活动中最热闹、最令人期待的环节，水花飞溅、百舸争流的激烈夺标场景，千姿百态、盛装出行的彩龙，都是人们久久难以忘怀的盛景。

赛龙斗标

佛山赛龙，规模不一，跨区跨县的龙舟可以参加大规模公开赛，同一村落内的兄弟龙舟也可以斗一斗。按照参与者的范围，佛山赛龙斗标分为两种：一是村落内部或契友兄弟村落之间的“围内制”赛，设置了参赛龙舟范围，参赛龙舟比较少，规模较小；二是“通天埠”龙舟公开赛，参与者不限于契友兄弟，而是面向全社会，地域上甚至要跨乡跨县，参与的龙舟多则上百条，少也有数十条，规模宏大。

契友兄弟或村落内部龙舟的斗标，规模较小，比赛是为了增

3.4 Enjoying the Dragon Boat Gala

There are two forms of the Dragon Boat Gala in Foshan, namely, the dragon boat race and the dragon boat pageant. While the race, also called by the locals as "vying for the prize", mainly focuses on speed, the pageant, also known as "gathering and cruising around" emphasizes decoration of the dragon boat and paddling skills. Among all the activities during the Dragon Boat Festival, the dragon boat gala comes out as the highlight, boasting such unforgettable spectacles as fierce competition among a myriad of dragon boats for the prize on splashing water, and the stunning cruises of magnificent dragon boats with various decorations.

Dragon Boat Races

Dragon boat races in Foshan vary in scale, ranging from village-level competitions to large-scale open tournaments with competitors from different counties and districts. Races, according to restrictions on participants, can be classified into two categories. One is contests within the village or among sworn brothers, which are small in scale with just a few competitors. The other is open tournaments, which welcome competitors from various townships and counties and as a result have dozens or even hundreds of dragon boats taking part.

The dragon boat races among sworn brothers or villagers are held to create an air of festivity, and enhance cohesion and connections among residents in the village. Under the circumstances, people care less about the results. Sometimes, this kind of race is regarded by competitors as a warm-up match or a trial for competitions at higher levels, which helps to build a competitive atmosphere, boost morale, and select qualified teams.

During traditional or folk festivals, such small-scale dragon boat races are held in pools or creeks in countless villages in Foshan. Though small in scale, races of different villages have their own characteristics. In Jianggen Village, Xi'nan Street, Sanshui District, its dragon boat race, usually organized during the Dragon Boat Festival, features three teams made up of three generations respectively, namely, the young, the middle-aged, and the elderly. Three age groups compete for the glory of the strongest generation. In Shangguanyuan Village of the same district, the dragon boat races still see the traditional custom of "releasing the dragons by cutting off the ropes". In other words, in order to prevent false-starts, dragon boats are tightly fastened by ropes until the commencing order is given. Different from common straight-course racing, dragon boat races in Gangtou Village, Baini Town take place in circles, which test the skills and stamina of the paddlers.

As tournaments are open to teams from various regions, they involve fierce competition and offer abundant rewards. Such large-scale races can only be held on a wide, gentle watercourse with large open ground space along the banks that can serve as the grandstand. Moreover, given the huge workload throughout the match, financing, and security, only extraordinary villages can afford to organize such events. In recent years, as dragon boat racing has flourished all over Foshan City, a lot of villages have hosted large-scale dragon boat races, such as Zhangcha in Chancheng District; Diejiao, Huangqi, Dongxiu, Xiebian, and Yayao in Nanhai District; Magang and Wanggang in Shunde District; and Baini in Sanshui District.

In general, a dragon boat race in Foshan consists of three sessions, namely, releasing the dragons, racing, and vying for the prize. Each dragon boat is equipped with a helmsman, a drummer, and paddlers. A gong player and a prize grabber are also included in a larger boat. Long dragon boats also have two drummers and two gong players, each with different responsibilities during the racing.

In the past, there were various ways to release the dragon boats in Foshan, one of which was by the helmsmen. This tradition is still preserved in Baini Town.

九江龙舟送阿契（九江文化站）
Jiujiang Dragon Boat Seeing its Sworn Brothers Off (Jiujiang Township Cultural Station)

添节日气氛，增强村庄的凝聚力，加深彼此之间的感情，比赛结果不是最重要的。有时候，这些比赛也可以看作是更大规模赛事前的热身赛或者选拔赛，有营造气氛、调动情绪、选拔参赛龙舟队的作用。

每年传统节日或民俗节日期间，佛山很多村落都会举办这种小规模的龙舟斗标，数条龙舟聚在一起，水塘中、河涌里就可以来一场热闹的龙舟赛。比赛规模不大，但各有特色。三水西南江根村有端午赛龙舟的传统，他们的比赛别出心裁，分别组成老、中、青三个年龄段的村民龙舟队，三代人同场竞技，看看哪代人能力强。西南上官员村龙舟赛还保留了“砍缆放龙”的古老习俗，龙舟起跑前用缆绳系住、绷紧，发令时同时砍断缆绳，防止龙舟“抢跑”。白坭岗头村龙舟赛与常见的直道竞速比赛不同，以绕圈竞速赛考验参赛选手的技巧与耐力。

“通天埠”龙舟公开赛，参与者不限于契友兄弟，而是广邀各地龙舟队伍参赛，参与的龙舟多则上百条，少也有数十条，规模宏大，比赛过程非常激烈，其奖品也比较丰厚。这样大规模的斗标比赛，要选择水流平缓、水面宽阔的河道，河道两边还要有大片空地，以供比赛时当作观众看台。赛前、赛中、赛后有大量的工作要做，资金和安全都不是小问题，不是一般的村落可以主办的。近年佛山各地扒龙舟运动发展得如火如荼，各村、镇、区都在积极承办大规模的龙舟斗标赛事，如禅城张槎，南海叠滘、黄岐、东秀、谢边、雅瑶，顺德马岗、旺岗，三水白坭等地，近几年来都有举办大规模的龙舟赛事。

佛山赛龙斗标一般有三个环节，即放龙、竞渡、抢标。斗标时，龙舟上配备的人员有舵手、鼓手、扒丁，比较大的龙舟还有锣手、标手等，长龙还备有两个鼓手、两个锣手，他们在竞渡时各有分工。

旧时，佛山放龙形式多样，其中一种叫舦公（舵手）放龙，如今三水白坭还保留着这种传统的放龙方式。通过抽签决定比赛顺序的龙舟呈一字形排列在江河上，而所有龙舟的舵手则集中在50~100米开外的岸上。号炮一响，比赛正式开始，舵手取令牌或彩带后，奋力向着自己的龙舟奔跑，急速上船，舵手上龙舟后，龙舟才能出发。瞬间百舸争流，你追我赶，场面极为壮观。现在比赛大都是在一排龙舟前设置一根红绸带或者彩色浮球，所有龙舟不得超出红绸

Before the race, dragon boats, whose positions are decided through drawing lots, are floating on the river side-by-side, in a straight horizontal line, with the helmsmen standing ashore 50 to 100 meters away from their boats. The event begins at the sound of the starting pistol. The helmsmen, after snatching their token or ribbon, rush to their boat, which cannot set off until its helmsman is on board. In an instant, all the dragon boats rush forward, striving to overtake one another. These days, a red ribbon or a string of colorful float balls are set before the dragon boats as the starting line. Paddlers row feverishly on hearing the starting pistol and the dragon boats are dashing forward amid resounding cheers and shouts from the crowds on the river banks.

At the beginning of the race, paddling is synchronized with the drumbeats at a steady pace. Halfway down the racecourse, the dragon boats begin to gain speed. In a sprint for the line, the drummer bows forward, raising the drumsticks high and pounding them on the drum as if he were going to break it. He musters up every single ounce of strength inside his body so as to exhort the paddlers to perform at their peak. Dong! Dong! Dong! Rapid drumbeats keep going on. In dragon boat racing, paddlers must row to the rhythm of the drum that is

白坭镇的舦公放龙

Helmsmen Releasing the Dragons in Baini Town

considered a command to them. Reminded and inspired by the drummer, the passionate and vigorous paddlers no longer sit on their seats, but go down on one knee, rowing with greater efforts amid roaring calls. Such intense competition was vividly portrayed by Zhang Jianfeng, a poet from the Tang Dynasty in his poem "Boat Race Song", which says, "With the rapid drumbeats the prize is approaching; eyes of two dragons are fixed on their prey. Shouts ashore seem louder than thunder; colorful flags aboard keep dazzling eyes. The faster boat grab their prey, leaving the one behind paddle in vain."

Vying for the prize occurs at the final stage of the dragon boat race. In the past, prize grabbers went for what was floating in the water, such as a fish, a duck, a goose, or a banknote. Such prizes were tied with red brocade, and therefore called the "brocade prize". Near the end of the racing, the prize grabber got fully prepared. When the boat was 20 meters away from the prize, he climbed and perched on the bow, hooking his feet under the side of the boat and bending forward. As soon as the boat reached the destination, the grabber jumped into

2013年国庆九江传统龙舟赛
Jiujiang Traditional Dragon Boat Race on National Day, 2013

带或彩色浮球所在之处，发令枪一响，扒丁就奋力划桨，龙舟如离弦之箭一般冲出去，瞬间，两岸黑压压的人群发出巨大的欢呼声和呐喊声，响彻云霄。

竞渡初始，鼓声和落扒速度均衡；赛程快过半时，龙舟速度就越来越快。进入冲刺阶段后，鼓手为了激励扒丁，身子弓向前，鼓槌高高举起又重重落下，大有将龙船鼓敲破的架势，“咚咚咚”急促的鼓声不绝于耳。鼓手拼尽全身力气的劲头，给予了扒丁们极大的鼓舞。划龙舟是“听鼓下桡”，鼓声就是命令，在鼓手的提醒和鼓舞下，扒丁们热血齐涌，干劲倍增，由先前的坐着划桨，一律改为跪着一条腿，弓着一条腿，半蹲半站式地拼命用力，发出了一声声怒吼般的号子声。唐代诗人张建封的《竞渡歌》将竞渡冲刺的激烈场面描写得非常生动：“鼓声渐急标将近，两龙望标目如瞬。坡上人呼霹雳惊，竿头彩挂虹蜺晕。前船抢水已得标，后船失势空挥桡。”

抢标是赛龙的结束阶段，旧时赛龙会抢浮标，如鱼标、鹅鸭标、钱标等，因其上系有红锦缎，所以也叫“锦标”。标手要提前做好准备，在离标20米处即需爬上船头，双脚勾着船舷，身向前倾。龙舟一到达终点，所有标手立刻跳进水里去抢标，第一个将标举过头顶的为胜者。现在赛龙没有抢标的环节了，大都是在终点处悬一红绸带或彩球，最先到达终点的龙舟，红绸带或彩球就会挂到其龙头上。

要想竞渡取得胜利，关键在于全船人员的通力合作。首先舵手要掌好舵，稳稳控制住龙舟前进的方向，不让龙舟偏离赛道，既不能妨碍其他龙舟，也不可偏向水岸，同时要利用自身重量做有韵律的运动巧妙地使龙舟头翘起，减少龙舟前进的阻力。此外，舵手还起助划的作用，因此舵手必须是经验丰富之人。

鼓手是整条龙舟的指挥，负责指挥扒丁落扒的频率和力度，鼓舞士气，控制着龙舟在起航、中途和冲刺等不同阶段的行进速度。一次赛龙，距离长的有数十千米，短的也有数百米，不可能全程保持一样的速度，这些都需要靠鼓手来调控。比赛中，锣手、鼓手均不得参与划桨。

龙舟上所有扒丁在鼓手的调配下，同时起扒落扒，身体前倾，胳膊上肌肉突出，嘴中发出“嗨嗬，嗨嗬”的号子声，富有力量

2013年国庆九江传统龙舟赛标部的美酒和烧猪
Trophies of Fine Wine and Roast Pork of Jiujiang Traditional Dragon Boat Race on National Day, 2013

龙舟盛会
Dragon Boat Gala

the water to snatch the prize. The first one who lifted the award over his head was the winner. Today, these floating prizes have been replaced by a red ribbon or a string of colorful balls hanging over the finishing line. The fastest dragon boat will get the prize hung on its head when crossing the line.

In the dragon boat race, the key to championship lies in cooperation among the crew. First of all, the helmsman should set a good direction for the dragon boat's movement, ensuring that it will not veer off the racecourse, running into other boats or going towards the banks. In the meatime, the helmsman should make rhythmic body movements, using his weight to raise the bow of the boat, which helps to reduce water resistance. In addition, a helmsman who facilitates paddling must be experienced.

The drummer is the commander of the whole boat, responsible for boosting morale and adjusting the pace throughout the race by setting the frequency and intensity for paddling. Since the distance of dragon boat races varies from hundreds to thousands of meters, it is impossible to maintain the same speed during the entire journey. Therefore, it is the responsibility of the drummer to set different paces for the boat in different stages. Drummers and gong players are forbidden from paddling during the competition.

Paddlers, led by the drummer, synchronize their paddling with each other while shouting "Hi Ho, Hi Ho", their bodies leaning forwards and their muscles on the arm bulging, which presents the beauty of strength. While racing, paddlers can either sit or kneel down. Rowing in a kneeling position makes the boat move faster than in a sitting one, for such a position enables paddlers to make use of their arms, waists and thighs together. However, the kneeling position is more difficult for paddlers in that it requires long-term training. Seasoned paddlers only stir up few splashes, with each paddling strong and steady, rushing the boat forward.

Dragon Boat Pageants

While dragon boat races are exhilarating and engaging, dragon boat pageants are eye-catching thanks to the colorful boats with varied appearances. The Dazhou Dragon Boat in Panyu District, is second to none in terms of its magnificence that is recorded in *New Notes on Guangdong* by Qu Dajun. According to his descriptions, the marvellous boat boasted a lifelike dragon head and tail, on which brilliant puppet shows were performed. In the spring of 1977, the Guangdong Provincial Administration of Cultural Relics discovered an ancient boat with complicated decorations in the sugarcane field 50 meters away from the east of the Dazhou Village. As its design and structure matches the descriptions in the aforementioned book, the boat has been identified as the Dazhou Dragon Boat, which in turn proves the authenticity of the account.

In a dragon boat pageant, it is beauty, not speed that plays a dominant role. During the dragon boat cruise, essential decorations on the boat are special umbrellas, gongs, drums, and flags which usually involve great care in order to make the boat stand out. The flags and umbrellas are mainly in red, but some yellow, orange, green, and blue. Moreover, there are auspicious patterns on the umbrellas, such as dragons, phoenixes, bats, and the Eight Immortals in the

感。竞渡时扒丁可以根据需要采用坐姿或跪姿，而使用跪姿时龙舟划行的速度非常快，所有人都手握桨并弯腰，手、腰、脚一起发力，龙舟一闪一闪向前疾冲。但是跪姿比较难，必须经过长期的训练才能用好。训练有素的扒丁起扒落扒只搅起很少的水花，一桨一桨沉稳扎实，推动龙舟飞速向前。

彩龙竞艳

龙舟竞渡，斗标生猛，惊险刺激，扣人心弦；彩龙竞艳，色彩艳丽，旖旎多姿，同样吸睛。广东最著名的彩龙要数番禺大洲龙船，屈大均在《广东新语》中有记载。从屈大均的记载可知，大洲龙船制作非常豪华，龙首、龙尾栩栩如生，船上还有精彩的傀儡戏表演，该彩龙设计之巧妙、制作之精美，令人叹为观止。1977年春，广东省文物管理处在番禺钟村大洲村以东50米的蔗田里发现了一艘古船，其装饰繁复，古船形制与上述文献对大洲龙船的描述一致，由此断定此古船就是大洲龙船，证明文献记述为真。

竞艳比赛在于竞美而非竞速。罗伞、锣、鼓、旗帜等是游龙必备的装饰，为了让自己村的龙舟出彩，人们会在这些必备装饰上大做文章。罗伞、彩旗颜色鲜艳，以红色调为主，配以黄色、橙色、绿色、蓝色等其他鲜艳的色彩。罗伞图案主要为各种吉祥图案，如龙、凤、蝙蝠、八仙等，装扮出鲜艳夺目、各有特色的彩龙，洋溢着喜庆的气氛。扒丁的衣服鞋帽必须统一，显得扒丁精神抖擞、神采奕奕。一些彩龙为了夺人眼球，除了设置传统的罗伞、彩旗等，

禅城张槎大江彩龙
Colorful Dragon of Dajiang, Zhangcha of Chancheng District

还会有别出心裁的设计：在龙船上表演各种节目，如上文中大洲龙船的傀儡戏，一些彩龙还会有飘色、舞龙、舞狮、打太极、十番等表演，让人大饱眼福。叠滘彩龙把当地民间器乐佛山十番搬上龙舟，长长的龙舟在狭窄弯曲的河涌上游动，船上的孩子们稳稳地站着表演十番的各种高难度动作，岸上的人们纷纷喝彩鼓掌。还有在龙舟上布置生活场景的，如：放置棋盘，让两位老者端坐对弈；设树根茶几，由两位老者品茗谈笑，闲话桑麻；设书桌和电脑，择一学童在其中上网。

Chinese legend. All the decorations make the dragon boats lively and energetic and create a festive atmosphere. On such occasions, paddlers are in the same uniforms to showcase their vigor. Apart from routine flags and umbrellas, some creative dragon boats have other unique designs. Various performances are specially put on aboard, such as puppet shows mentioned before, the *piaose* (flying dance of children dressed in ancient costumes), dragon dances, lion dances, Taiji, and Shifan music (a series of melodies played with around ten folk musical instruments), presenting a feast for the eye. For instance, on the colorful dragon boat of Diejiao Village, the Shifan music is played by children, who make difficult movements aboard in a stable manner while the long dragon boat is moving on the narrow meandering creek, winning cheers and applause from people ashore. Scenes of life are displayed on some other boats, such as two elders playing Chinese chess beside a chessboard, or enjoying tea and chatting by a tea table made of a tree stump; or a student surfing the Internet with a laptop at a desk.

彩龙巡游
Cruise of Colorful Dragon Boats

Boats should move slowly in the pageant to leave enough time for the spectators to appreciate. Therefore, paddlers generally row in a gentle manner. Sometimes, a few people will stand on the bow and stern, stamping forcefully, which helps the boat move forward rhythmically on splashing water. The more audience on the banks, the more rapturous their cheers and applause are, and the more rhythmically paddlers row. Once encountering a familiar dragon boat, a water fight may start between the two boats just for fun. Then there are times when the capsizing of one boat stirs up a cry of surprise from the crowds. In the past, there were also stunt performances during dragon boat pageants in Jiujiang, such as the afore-mentioned turning of the umbrella on Zhongzhou Dragon Boat and flying of the gong on Zhongshan Dragon Boat. Unfortunately, such exclusive stunts can no longer be performed by anyone.

彩龙竞艳不竞速，因此其行进速度较慢，有利于岸上观众尽情欣赏龙舟的“盛世美颜”。扒丁们缓缓地划动龙舟，有时船头船尾还各站立几人，用力踩踏，使龙舟有节奏地、欢快地行进，水花飞溅。岸上的观众越多，喝彩鼓掌声越热烈，扒丁们就会将龙舟划得更有节奏感。身边有熟悉的龙舟划过时，人们就会互相打水仗逗趣，有龙舟被打翻了，引得岸上的人群阵阵惊呼。旧时九江游龙还会有绝活表演，如前文已提及的中洲罗伞、忠山锣，可惜现在已无人能表演了。

第五节 洗（喝）龙舟水

洗（喝）龙舟水防病治病是一种水疗巫术，有着合理的心理因素，此习俗流布广泛。在早期人类社会，人们认为生病是由于妖怪、精灵或灵物等神秘力量在起作用，因此只要赶走妖怪或精灵等神秘力量，病人自能痊愈。水作为一种重要的自然物质，它具有清洁、去污的功能，它能够去除物质表面的污垢。根据类似的原理，人们就认为水也可以赶走精灵、妖魔等，水被应用到治病巫术中，形成了各种各样的水疗巫术。

以水为药的水疗巫术在中国各民族中广泛存在。如西南彝族人如果有发烧、发炎、霍乱等症，巫师就要上山找“仙水”，取下来给病人喝下去治病。所谓仙水，实质上就是雨后土坑中的积水。海南岛黎族人信仰“龙泉”，认为龙泉是神仙饮过的泉水，或说此泉为龙饮水之处，其水可以治病，可以供神，有驱邪逐魔的神力。佛山和邻县乡民历来习惯在农历七月初七灌储“七夕水”，据说“七夕水”久储不腐，人们把它当作平时的清凉饮料，特别是病人的饮用水。

洗（喝）龙舟水在粤地比较流行，粤地大部分地区有洗（喝）龙舟水的习俗，康熙《新宁县志》《开平县志》均有记载。康熙

3.5 Bathing in and Drinking Dragon Boat Water

Bathing in and drinking dragon boat water to prevent and cure diseases is a kind of spiritual hydrotherapy. This custom spreads widely with reasonable psychological factors. In early human society, people considered that diseases were caused by some mysterious forces like monsters, spirits or supernatural beings of witchcraft so patients would recover by driving those things away. As an important natural material, water has the function of decontamination, which means that it can remove the dirt on the surfaces. According to similar principles, people think that water is able to ward off evil. Water is therefore applied to spiritually cure diseases, forming various types of spiritual hydrotherapy.

洗龙舟水
Bathing in Dragon Boat Water

Spiritual hydrotherapy is widespread among different ethnic groups in China. For example, if the Yi people, mostly distributed in southwest China, suffer from fever, inflammation, cholera, or other diseases, the wizard will go into the hills for so-called celestial water (which is actually rain water in pits) for the patients to drink to cure them. The Li people in Hainan Province believe in the "dragon spring", thinking it to be a drinking place for the deities or the dragons, so it can be used to cure people and to be offered to gods because of its power of exorcism. People in Foshan and the nearby counties have had the custom of storing "Double Seventh Water" on the 7th day of the 7th lunar month, which can supposedly last a long time without deteriorating and be used as a normal cool drink, especially as the drinking water of patients.

The custom of bathing in and drinking dragon boat water has been quite popular in Guangdong Province since the ancient times. There are records of them in *Xinning County Chronicle* and *Kaiping County Chronicle* in the Kangxi period of the Qing Dynasty. According to the *Xinning County Chronicle*, during the Dragon Boat Festival, people made Zongzi (a Chinese rice-dumpling), drank realgar wine, calamus wine and absinthe, hung the Chinese mugwort on the door and held dragon boat races in the river, where spectators bathed themselves. After the dragon boat cruising and racing, especially between 11 a.m. and 1 p.m. on the fifth day of the fifth lunar month, villagers in Foshan rush to the river where the races have taken place to take a shower or wash their faces to pray for happines and well-being. Children are usually taken by their family members to wash their hands and feet in the "dragon boat water" as it can allegedly chase away evils and cure skin diseases and help them grow healthily. In the past, people would drink dragon boat water, wishing to drive away evil forces and to stay healthy. In ancient times, people in Chaoyang County also had this custom, which is recorded as, "When the Dragon Boat Festival comes, dragon boat races last for nearly a month. People honor those who win, and drink dragon boat water." However, due to the increasing awareness of personal hygiene, people seldom drink dragon boat water now.

洗龙舟水
Bathing in Dragon Boat Water

《新宁县志》云："端午酿黍角，饮雄黄、菖蒲艾酒，插艾虎于门，江浒设龙舟竞渡，往观者多于江上盥浴。"游龙、赛龙之后，特别是五月初五午时，佛山村民也会争先恐后地跳进龙舟划过的河中洗澡或在河涌边洗脸，以期沾一沾龙舟的灵气，祈求幸福安康。尤其是家中有小孩子的，家人通常都会把他们的小手小脚浸浸"龙舟水"，人们认为洗龙舟水可以辟除邪气，不生皮肤病，使孩子健康成长。旧时人们甚至还会喝几口龙舟水，祈求祛除身上的晦气邪气，保佑身体健康。旧时潮阳县也有喝龙舟水的习俗："（端午）自此，江浒竞渡几一月，夺标者咸以为荣，且有汲龙船水饮之者。"现在由于人们的卫生意识增强了，已很少喝龙舟水了。

第六节　吃龙舟饭

“龙舟饭”也称“龙舟宴”，是佛山龙舟文化的一部分。吃过龙舟饭，寓意一年顺利平安、五谷丰登。龙舟活动期间，佛山各村落都会组织一场场热闹的龙舟宴，亲朋兄弟契友、同村同宗村民欢聚一堂，在享用美酒美食时共话亲情友情，绝对是佛山水乡人心中最温馨的画面。有村民说，过年只是一家人团聚，而吃龙舟饭则是同村村民、亲戚朋友成百上千人相聚一起，场面的确比过年还要

龙舟饭
Dragon Boat Meal

3.6 Eating Dragon Boat Meals

The dragon boat meal, also known as the dragon boat banquet, is part of Foshan dragon boat culture. Having a dragon boat meal symbolizes a year of peace, security and abundant harvests. During the dragon boat activities, villages across Foshan will hold grand banquets, so that friends and relatives, sworn brothers, clan members and villagers gather together to enjoy wine and food, renewing their kinship ties and friendship with each other. That is definitely the warmest scene in the hearts of Foshan people. According to some villagers, the Spring Festival is just a time for family reunion, while the dragon boat banquet, where hundreds of people gather together, is doubtlessly livelier. Moreover, the scale of the banquet and the variety of dishes reflect the social connections and prosperity of a village. Therefore, people attach great importance to the preparation of the dragon boat meal, trying to serve more dishes and invite more guests. In Diejiao, Nanhai, some villages have the saying of "one chimney", which means that all the villagers enjoy the banquet together during the dragon boat activities without having to cook their own meals. Residents of other villages or tourists are also invited.

During the Dragon Boat Festival activities people can have dragon boat meals from the lifting to the hiding of dragon boats. When the dragon boat is to be lifted, members of the dragon boat club begin discussing related activities, such as the maintenance of the dragon boat, the purchase of dragon boat items, division of labor, the scale of the dragon boat race, visits to relatives and invitations of sworn brothers to the dragon boat meals, budgets and financing.

To facilitate those discussions, members need to have meals together at the ancestral hall. In addition, paddlers usually practice in advance, hoping to win

九江吃龙舟饭（九江文化站）
Eating Dragon Boat Meal at Jiujiang (Jiujiang Township Cultural Station)

the race. They train so hard that it's reasonable to treat them to dragon boat meals. Given the small number of people involved, the meal for the paddlers is very simple. In the past, dragon boat meals were prepared in a big pot and served in a big wooden barrel, and then sent to the paddlers by a special boat. Today the dragon boat meals are prepared by villagers. Though there are only five or six dishes, the portion should be big enough for the paddlers to eat their fill. The scale of these dragon boat meals is rather small since they are served mainly to members of the dragon boat club and the paddlers, not to non-participants in the activities.

The grandest dragon boat meal is held at noon or in the evening on the day of the dragon boat gala. It is this kind of dragon boat banquet that Qu Dajun once described, "When the winning team returns to its village, friends and relatives are called to feast, heralding a year of abundance, happiness and flourishing trade". Dragon boat meals of this kind have the largest number of participants including

热闹。而且龙舟饭的气氛热烈程度和菜肴丰盛与否，反映了一个村落人际交往和兴旺程度，因此人们对做好龙舟饭非常重视，尽量让菜肴更丰盛、邀请更多的客人来吃龙舟饭。南海叠滘一些村落还有“一支烟囱”的说法，在龙舟节活动期间，村中男女老少都不在家中开伙，都去吃龙舟饭，外村人或游客也会被邀请去吃龙舟饭。

从起龙到藏龙的整个龙舟节活动期间，都可以吃龙舟饭。开始起龙了，龙船会的人就要商量当年龙舟活动的诸多事项，如龙舟维修保养、龙舟物品购置、人员分工、龙舟赛规模、探亲和邀请契友吃龙舟饭、费用预算和筹资等。为了方便大家一起商量这些事宜，就需要在祠堂开伙一起吃龙舟饭。为了赛出好成绩，扒丁通常都会提前进行训练。训练非常辛苦，请扒丁吃龙舟饭慰劳一番是很有必要的。扒丁人数不多，吃的龙舟饭也简单，以前是做成大锅饭，盛进大木桶，由专门的艇仔送给扒丁吃。现在就请本村的人来做，菜式五六个，但要分量足、好下饭，让扒丁都能吃饱。这些龙舟饭的规模比较小，主要是龙船会的人和扒丁来吃，其他没有参加龙舟活动的人是不会来吃的。

最热闹、最盛大的龙舟饭在龙舟盛会当天的中午或晚上举行，这也是屈大均所说的“宴饮”，“斗得全胜还埠，则广召亲朋宴饮，其埠必年丰人乐、贸易以饶云”。此次吃龙舟饭的人范围最广，包括了全村男女老幼、兄弟契友、外来客人。以前经济条件一般的村落，都是龙舟饭做好后，村中男女老少到祠堂去领，领了一定分量的龙舟饭，回家跟自家饭煮在一起，让全家人都沾沾好运。现在是全村男女老少和客人欢聚一堂，一起享用美味吉祥的龙舟

思親念祖故鄉華嶺永留
FSTV

茶基村何氏祠堂龙舟饭
Dragon Boat Meal at the He Clan Ancestral Hall of Chaji Village

饭。龙舟盛会这天，会有外人和游客来到村中看龙舟赛，某些村落还会给看龙舟赛的人派发龙舟饭。领龙舟饭的人可以封个红包给对方，不封红包也没关系。现在可以向组织者预订龙舟饭，不论户籍不论身份，只要下订就可以吃到龙舟饭。现在龙舟饭的规模也越来越大，几百人的龙舟宴很常见，几千人、上万人同食龙舟饭也不鲜见。2008年和2010年，顺德都主办了大型的“万人龙舟宴”，用于推广顺德的龙舟文化和美食文化。活动现场，30多名顺德名厨亲临现场主理，500多名工作人员为食客服务，万余人围坐在上千餐桌前大块朵颐，场面非常壮观。

以前佛山经济水平一般，大多数村落不富裕，龙舟饭也简单，都是请本村落的厨师和妇女来做，有空闲的人也可以来帮忙。现在还有一些村落由本村人为大家做龙舟饭，但大多数村落都是请流动餐馆做龙舟饭，流动餐馆不仅包买食材、烹饪，还包碗筷、桌椅板凳和餐后卫生，非常省心。有的干脆去酒店预定龙舟饭，更加省事方便。

龙舟饭的最初目的是犒劳扒丁，让他们吃了龙舟饭后更有力气划龙舟，最简单的做法是将大米、腊肉、菜干等做成一锅香，特别“撑肚子”。食材都是各家各户提供的，东家一条腊肉、西家几斤米，凑足材料就可以做成一大锅龙舟饭。后来又多了几个本地菜，加上扒丁得到的烧猪、白酒等，龙舟饭逐渐丰富起来。近年来，佛山各地龙舟饭菜式越来越丰富，不同村落各有特点。

南海九江的龙舟饭要九菜一汤，榄角烧肉、酸梅鹅、姜葱大头鱼、芋头煮猪肉、青菜等都是龙舟饭中的常见菜。龙舟饭随时代不

all the villagers, friends and sworn brothers, and guests from outside the village. In the past, villages that were not rich would have the dragon boat meals cooked in the ancestral hall and have them brought back home and cooked by the villagers together with their own meals so that the whole family could have good luck. Today villagers gather with guests to share a delicious and auspicious dragon boat meal. On the day of the dragon boat gala, outsiders and tourists visit the village to watch the dragon boat race, and some villages even distribute dragon boat meals to visitors who could return the kindness with a red envelope sealed with money. But it's optional. Anyone, regardless of where he or she is from, can now order dragon boat meals from the organizer. The scale of dragon boat meals is getting larger and larger. Dragon boat banquets for hundreds of people are very common. It is not rare to see thousands of or tens of thousands of people enjoy dragon boat meals together. In 2008 and 2010 respectively, Shunde hosted a large-scale "Dragon Boat Banquet for Ten Thousand People" to promote its dragon boat culture and food culture. Over 30 renowned chefs in Shunde attended the events, together with more than 500 staff members serving more than 10,000 people who enjoyed themselves at over a thousand tables. It was quite an extraordinary scene.

In the past, Foshan's economy was not well developed and most villages were not rich, so dragon boat meals were simple. They were made by cooks and women in the village, and those who were free could come to help. In some villages, the dragon boat meals are still prepared by villagers while in most others mobile restaurants are hired for the sake of convenience. These restaurants not only purchase ingredients and do the cooking, but also provide tableware, chairs and tables, and post-dinner cleaning. Some villages simply order dragon boat meals at restaurants, which is more convenient.

The original purpose of the dragon boat meals was to reward the paddlers, so that they had more strength to paddle after the meals. The simplest method was to cook rice, preserved meat, and dried vegetables in a big pot, which could "easily fill the stomach". The ingredients were provided by different households. When all the needed materials were collected, a big pot of dragon boat meal would be made. Later, a few more local dishes were added, together with the roast pork and liquor won by the paddlers, enriching the dragon boat meals. In recent years, dishes served at the dragon boat banquets across Foshan have become even more abundant, with different characteristics in different villages.

The dragon boat meal in Jiujiang, Nanhai consists of nine dishes and one soup. Roast Pork with Preserved Olive, Stewed Goose in Plum Sauce, Steamed Fish with Ginger and Scallion, Stewed Pork with Taro and green vegetables are common dishes in the dragon boat meal. Though the dragon boat meal is improving as time goes by, Roast Pork with Preserved Olive still appears at the table of nearly every village as it symbolizes the hope of villagers to stand out and distinguish themselves because of the homonymy in the name of the dish in Chinese. In times of poverty, preserved olive was the main ingredient of this dish. Now with the improved living standard, the portion of roast pork has increased.

In the old days, people in Yanbu, Nanhai used large copper pots to serve the dragon boat meals with ingredients collected from different households. The meal was therefore named "Hundred-Household Dish". The ingredients included white beans, peppers, dried radishes, diced pork and so on. In recent years, the dragon boat meal is served on plates instead of in big pots. In addition to common dishes such as chicken, duck, fish and eggs, "Hundred-Household Dish" and Steamed Peppers with Garlic are a must. The former is a traditional dragon boat dish, reminding people of the hard old days. The latter is to eliminate the internal dampness of the paddlers. Autumn eggplant is a specialty of Yanbu, and a recommended dish in its dragon boat meal, which is very popular among guests.

Shunde's gastronomic culture is well-known at home and abroad, The food has won high praise for its freshness and tenderness. The dragon boat meal in Shunde highlights the characteristics of the local delicacies. In 2008, the "Dragon Boat Banquet for Ten Thousand People" held in Shunde consisted of 11 "best-recommended dishes", such as Five-Colored Dragon Boat Rice, Duck Soup with White Gourd and Coix Seeds, Braised Goose with Sweet Vinegar Sauce, Hometown Spiced Pork, Phoenix City Pork Roll and Fried Milk, Braised Eel with Pomelo Peel and Garlic, Fried Pine with Diced Meat and Vegetables,

断改进，但无论是哪个村落，大都有榄角烧肉这一道菜，寓意“榄角榄角，出头露角”，希望村人出人头地。贫困时期，榄角是这一道菜的主角，现在经济条件越来越好，烧肉的份量就多起来了。

南海盐步人过去用大铜盆装龙舟菜，其菜式为“百家菜”，配料包括白豆、辣椒、干萝卜、肥猪肉粒等。近年来，大盆菜改成了碟菜，除了鸡、鸭、鱼、蛋等常见菜肴，“百家菜”和蒜蓉蒸辣椒是必上的。“百家菜”是传统龙舟饭菜式，提醒现在的人要忆苦思甜，蒜蓉蒸辣椒是为了驱除“扒仔”（即扒丁）身上的湿气。秋茄是盐步的特产，也是每年盐步龙舟饭的招牌菜肴，深受宾客青睐。

顺德美食文化驰名中外，其清鲜爽嫩滑的特色让人赞不绝口，顺德龙舟饭的菜式凸显了顺德美食的风味特点。2008年顺德“万人龙舟宴”的菜式由五色龙舟饭、冬瓜薏米煲水鸭、秘制彭公鹅、家乡五香肉、风城野鸡卷拼炸奶、柚皮蒜子鳝、松子雀巢丁、鸿运四杯鸡等11道顺德金牌菜组成，鸡鸭鹅肉一样不少。这些菜式也是有讲究的，家乡五香肉，祛湿补盐加开胃；松子雀巢丁，寓意人丁兴旺；烧鸡和烧鹅的皮都是

顺德龙眼村龙舟饭
Dragon Boat Meal of Longyan Village, Shunde

红色的，寓意龙船手身体健壮，能旗开得胜；薏米冬瓜汤则可以消暑祛湿。

高明荷城街道东亨村的龙舟饭，鸡鸭鱼肉也是必备的，其中“龙船肉”是东亨村的特色菜品。龙船肉其实就是扣肉，经过细火慢炆后，扣肉变得入口即化，肥而不腻，搭配上东亨村特制的酸瓜，吃起来很开胃。

龙舟饭的意义远远超过了吃饭本身，据老人们讲，吃过龙舟饭，成年人会龙精虎猛、身体健康，而小孩子吃了会矫健壮实、聪明伶俐。所以每逢龙舟节，在外打工、旅居外地的村民都会回到村中吃龙舟饭，还有一些外村人或游客也会去吃龙舟饭，讨个“好意头”。正因如此，龙舟饭绝不会浪费，多准备的龙舟饭大家会竞拍打包回家第二天继续吃，甚至剩余的茶叶、食材也会被人们买下带回家。

and Lucky Chicken with Four Cups of Sauces. But the dishes are not selected randomly. Hometown Spiced Pork eliminates internal dampness, supplements salt and whet the appetite. Fried Pine Nuts with Diced Meat and Vegetables symbolizes a flourishing family. The skins of chicken and goose are roasted brownish, symbolizing that paddlers are strong-built, capable of success in the competitions. Soup With White Gourd and Coix Seeds can relieve summer heat and eliminate internal dampness.

Chicken, duck, fish and pork are also indispensable at the dragon boat banquet in Dongheng Village, Hecheng Street, Gaoming District. "Dragon Boat Meat" is the village's special dish, which is actually braised pork. The meat is simmered so soft that it melts in the mouth, fat but not greasy. It is really appetizing when served with the village's special pickled cucumber.

The meaning of the dragon boat meal is far beyond the meal itself. The elderly say that adults who have eaten the meal will be energetic and healthy and children will be strong and smart. Therefore, during the Dragon Boat Festival, villagers working and living outside all return to the village to have dragon boat meals, together with residents of other villages or tourists who want to share their luck. It is for this reason that the food will never be wasted. People bid for the extra food, wrap it up and take it home to eat the next day. They even buy the spare tea and ingredients.

3.7 Separating and Hiding the Dragon Boat

After the dragon boat racing and meals, villages in Foshan start separating and hiding their dragons. The head, the tail and the decorations are stored in the ancestral hall, temple or clubhouse, which is called separating the dragon. The storage of the dragon body depends on its materials. The traditional Pontianak wood dragon boat will crack due to dryness so it must be buried in the mud. The China fir dragon boat needs to be stored in a cool, dry and well-ventilated place, mostly in the clubhouse or ancestral hall. An auspicious date must be chosen to hide the dragon. First the villagers go to worship the deities in the temple, with firecrackers, incenses, candles and other sacrificial items before they hide the dragon boat. The hiding place is called the dragon bed, where there should be little pollution, good water, and preferably a lot of decaying plants to protect the dragon boat and make it shine. Some villages hide their dragon boats in the mud of the river, while others in ponds. To hide it in the river, first a pit is formed with sandbags. Then after the boat is pushed into it, the opening is covered with

藏龙舟
Hiding the Dragon Boat

第七节　散龙和藏龙

杉木龙舟藏在室内
China Fir Dragon Boat Stored Indoors

赛完龙舟，吃罢龙舟饭，佛山各村就陆续散龙和藏龙了。龙舟身上的各种装饰、龙头、龙尾和龙舟身是分开保存的，龙头、龙尾和龙舟装饰等要存放到祠堂、庙宇或会所中，这就是散龙。龙舟身的存放要依龙舟的材质来定，传统坤甸木龙舟会因干燥而开裂，必须埋藏到淤泥中。杉木龙舟则需要存放在阴凉干燥通风的房屋里，多存放在会所或祠堂中。藏龙也要挑日子，先到村中庙宇去拜神，鞭炮、香烛等祀神用品是必不可少的，然后再藏龙舟。藏龙舟的地方叫作龙床，必须污染少、水质好，淤泥中最好含有比较多的腐烂植物，这样的淤泥能滋养龙舟，龙舟会变得漆黑发亮。有的村落将龙舟藏在河涌淤泥中，也有沉埋在池塘中的。在河涌中藏龙舟，要先用沙包围成一个坳，将龙舟推进去后拿沙包封住坳口，在坳里面插几根竹子作为标记，再把龙舟上的活动塞拔开让船身沉入水中，也有用沙包压沉龙舟将其藏于水底的。在池塘中藏龙舟，先将龙舟划到预定沉埋的位置，插上几根竹子做标记，再拔掉龙舟底部的塞子，让水慢慢进入，龙舟则随之逐渐沉入水中。

在佛山民间习俗中，龙舟就是一条真龙，所以在藏龙过程中也有不少讲究，如藏龙舟不能说埋龙舟或沉龙舟等。

sandbags. Some bamboos are inserted in the pit as marks and the piston of the boat is unplugged so that it sinks to the bottom of water. Some dragon boats are filled with sandbags to sink to the bottom of the river. To hide the dragon boat in the pond, the boat is first rowed to the predetermined position, and then some bamboos are inserted as marks. After that, the piston at the bottom of the boat is unplugged to let in water slowly to make it submerge in water.

In Foshan folk customs, the dragon boat is equivalent to a real dragon, so there are a lot of taboos during the dragon boat hiding process. For example, one cannot say bury or sink the dragon boat.

FOSHAN

第四章 村落龙舟 精彩纷呈

Chapter 4 Unique and Colorful Village Dragon Boats

佛山各地的龙舟制造与装饰、龙舟活动礼仪和程序有很多共同之处，但十里不同风、百里不同俗，佛山各村落因为文化、习俗、自然环境等的差异，其龙舟文化各有特色，精彩纷呈。

The dragon boat building and decoration, rituals and procedures in various places of Foshan have a lot in common, but at the same time, because of their different cultures, customs and natural surroundings, the dragon boat culture in each village is unique and colorful.

赛龙舟
Dragon Boat Race

4.1 Dragon Boat Cruises in Dajiang Village, Zhangcha

Dajiang (Big River) Village is located to the southwest of Zhangcha Street, Chancheng, Foshan. In ancient times there was a big river running through it, which was connected to the Dongping River and the Fenjiang River, hence its name. The village belonged to Nanhai County. With densely distributed creeks, the village has had the tradition of dragon boating during the Dragon Boat Festival over the past centuries. Because of the narrow and curved creeks, cruises of colorful dragon boats are held instead of dragon boat races or competitions for trophies. During the Dragon Boat Festival, dressed-up dragon boats meander in the creeks of Dajiang Village. People from different villages all gather on both banks of the creeks to watch the colorful dragon boats. In the village, both the Feng and Luo clans have colorful dragon boats. The Fengs' boats have cruised their colorful dragon boats during each Dragon Boat Festival for the past three decades but the Luos have not done so for over a decade. The Fengs have also been invited to perform and compete in the Fenjiang River, the Dongping River and the Pearl River and have won a number of awards. In 2015, the colorful dragon boat custom of the Fengs of Dajiang Village was listed as an intangible cultural heritage of Foshan City.

The unique natural environment of Dajiang Village contributes to its custom of dragon boat cruises, whose procedural ritual is complete and unique, including entering the water, renovating, collecting the greens, eating dragon boat meals, lifting the dragon, dotting the eyes, decorating, cruising, visiting relatives and hiding the dragon.

The Fengs' colorful dragon boat is made of China fir and stored within the dragon welcoming gate on the right of the Feng Clan Ancestral Hall. The

第一节　张槎大江　游龙戏水

大江村位于佛山禅城张槎街道西南面，古时此处有大江河与东平河、汾江河连通，遂以大江为村名，属南海县。大江为水乡，河涌密布，数百年来都有端午划龙舟的传统。因村内河涌狭窄多弯，故很少举办赛龙斗标，多是彩龙巡游。每当端午时节，盛装打扮的彩龙在大江村的河涌中蜿蜒前进，十里八乡的人们聚集在河涌两岸，争相一睹大江彩龙的神韵。大江村内冯氏家族和罗氏家族都有彩龙，罗氏彩龙十多年未见巡游戏水，冯氏近30年来每逢端午节都举办彩龙巡游，还多次受邀前往汾江河、东平河、珠江参加表演和比赛，获得数个奖项。2015年大江冯氏彩龙习俗被评为佛山市市级非物质文化遗产项目。

冯氏世祠
The Feng Clan Ancestral Hall

大江村因为独特的自然环境，形成了游龙戏水的风俗习惯，其彩龙巡游的程序礼仪完整而别具一格，包括龙舟落水、整修、采青、吃龙舟饭、起龙、点睛、装饰、巡游、探亲、藏龙等。

冯氏彩龙为杉木制造，平时就收藏在冯氏世祠右边的接龙门内。一般在农历五月初一这天的午饭后，龙舟举行落水仪式。吉时一到，龙舟扒丁开始敲锣打鼓，三两妇人在接龙门门口焚香祭祀、拜神祈福。冯氏彩龙长22.8米、重达2吨，以前要上百人才能抬起，然后缓缓拖到祠堂前的风水塘中，并让水漫进船厢，这就是彩龙落水。因龙舟在接龙门内沉睡了一年，木板间的缝隙变宽，只有在水中浸泡几天后才适合游龙。现在接龙门内设置了轨道，只需十几人就可以把龙舟推出来，众人先用绳子绑紧龙舟，再用吊车缓缓地把龙舟吊至风水塘内。据村民透露，每年农历五月初一举办彩龙落水仪式时，锣鼓声响起后总会下起雨来，据说是龙在沉睡一年后苏醒并要出来了，就会牵动风云，带来“龙舟水”。

五月初五的清晨，冯氏长者出门采青了，采青的长者要丁财两旺、身体健康且高寿，所采之青为黄皮叶，还必须是开过花结过果的黄皮树叶。黄皮叶采回来后，长者将部分黄皮叶煮水，用一条新毛巾蘸黄皮叶水擦拭龙头、龙尾，最后将剩余的黄皮叶用红绳子稳稳地绑在龙角上。

五月初一中午龙舟落水后，参与活动的人中午一般会聚在一起吃龙舟饭。但参与人数最多、规模最大的龙舟饭还是五月初五端午节龙舟巡游前中午和巡游后晚上的龙舟饭，遇到大办年份就更加热闹。在大办年份，五月初五中午的龙舟饭，会邀请参与龙舟活动的扒丁、龙船会成员、村中老人（男60岁以上，女55岁以上），还

祭龙
Worshipping the Dragon

ceremony for the dragon boat to enter water usually takes place after lunch of the first day of the fifth lunar month. When the auspicious time comes, the paddlers start beating the drums and gongs while several women burn incenses at the gate to pray for good luck. The Fengs' colorful dragon boat is 22.8 meters long and as heavy as 2 tons. In the past it took more than a hundred people to lift and carry it slowly to the Fengshui Pond in front of the temple to submerge it into water. This is the ritual of dragon boat entering water. As the dragon boat has been lying within the dragon welcoming gate for a whole year, there are greater seams between the planes. It has to be submerged in the water for a few days before it is suitable for cruising. Nowadays, rails are installed in the dragon welcoming gate, so only a dozen people suffice to push the dragon boat out. The dragon boat is tied with ropes and hoisted by a crane to the Fengshui Pond. According to the villagers, there is always rain after beating the drums and gongs at the dragon-entering-water ceremony. It is said that after sleeping for a year, the dragon will stir the wind and clouds when it comes out, bringing along "the dragon boat rain".

In the early morning of the fifth day of the fifth lunar month, the elders of the Fengs go out to collect the greens. These people must boast a big and prosperous family, good health and longevity. What they collect are leaves of wampee trees that have flowered and borne fruits. The elders cook some of the collected leaves and use the water to clean the dragon head and tail with a new towel and tie the remaining ones on the dragon horns with red strings.

After the dragon boat enters the water, all participants have dragon boat lunch together. But the biggest meals with the largest numbers of people are the lunch and the dinner before and after the cruise on the fifth day of the fifth lunar month. In years when there are grand celebrations, the meals are even more fascinating. At lunch, the paddlers, members of the dragon boat club, elders (men over 60 and women over 55), relatives of the Fengs in downtown and Huadu District of Guangzhou, and Gaoming and Sanshui of Foshan are invited to have a gathering together. In the evening, all the villagers have dinner together. As many as 270 to 280 tables are laid in and out of the ancestral hall for over 2,000 people to enjoy the meal together, which is a very lively scence.

After having the dragon boat lunch, the Fengs start lifting and decorating the dragon boat. After being submerged in water for a few days, the boat is filled with water, which has to be scooped out to lift the dragon boat to the surface. Then the dragon head, tail, drums and gongs, special umbrellas, and colorful flags are installed. The Fengs' dragon boat is luxuriously decorated. The head and the tail are carved from camphor wood, lacquered in gold and decorated with a yellow beard. The horns are tilted high and the mouth is wide open with its tongue sticking out. There is a drum with a diameter of 80 cm, bigger than an ordinary one. The drum sends out a resonant sound. Auspicious flowers and plants are painted on the side of the drum. The middle of the dragon card is embroidered with the Chinese characters of "Dajiang Shiping Feng", showing the family name and origin, which are surrounded by auspicious patterns such as deer, lions, peonies, plum blossoms, phoenixes and magpies. The lower brim of the card is decorated with yellow, red and white tassels. There are four performance flags, each of which is about two meters long in three colors of red, green and yellow. There are six special umbrellas, on which there are auspicious patterns of dragons, phoenixes, lions, the Eight Immortals, plum blossoms and peonies. There are four big flags in two specifications. The larger ones are over 10 meters long, which are only used when the dragon is cruising in the Fengshui Pond or in the creeks of the village because the wind and waves will be too strong for them in the Fenjiang River or the Dongping River. The smaller ones are about five to six meters long in three colors of red, yellow and green, on which auspicious words are embroidered. These are the flags often used during the dragon boat cruise. In recent years, in answer to the call of the municipal and district governments to promote Foshan's cultural and economic development,

有广州市区、花都，佛山高明、三水等地的冯氏宗亲参加，大家欢聚一堂。当日晚上大江冯氏男女老少所有村民吃龙舟饭，人数多时有270~280桌，2000多人一起吃饭。每到这天，祠堂内外摆满了桌椅，数千人一起吃龙舟饭，气氛非常热烈。

吃过中午的龙舟饭，冯氏就开始起龙和装饰龙舟。龙舟在风水塘中浸泡了几天，船内都是水，人们就将船里的水舀出来，使龙舟浮上水面，然后安装龙头、龙尾、锣鼓、罗伞、彩旗等装饰。冯氏彩龙装饰豪华，龙头、龙尾为樟木雕刻而成，金漆黄须，丫角高翘，张口见舌。锣鼓一套，鼓直径有80厘米，比一般的赛龙鼓直径要大，声音洪亮，鼓四周绘有吉祥花草。龙牌中间绣有“大江始平冯”字样，四周绣有鹿、狮子、牡丹、梅花、凤鸟、喜鹊等吉祥图案，下坠黄、红、白三色流苏。表演旗四面，两米左右长，有红、绿、黄三种颜色。罗伞六把，其上有龙、凤、狮子、八仙、梅花、牡丹等吉祥图案。大旗四面，有两种规格，一种10多米长，因为江河中风大浪大，10多米的大旗只是在村前风水塘或村内河涌巡游时才会带上船，去汾江河、东平河游龙一般不会装饰这种规格的大旗；另一种规格的大旗五六米长，有红、黄、绿等颜色，上面分别绣有“独占群龙”“海国称雄”“百桡”“风云际会”等字样，是游龙时经常会使用的大旗。头牌、罗伞、幡旗这些装饰都是在广州状元坊戏服厂购买的。近年来，为了响应市、区各级政府宣传佛山文化和经济建设的号召，冯氏请来佛山民间艺术社帮忙装饰龙舟，用金属做骨架，外面套上防水布制作的龙头龙尾，以及代表佛山文化的通济桥、祖庙、黄飞鸿、粤剧人物和代表佛山经济建设的佛山新媒体产业园、禅西新城等造型，这些现代装饰让人眼前一亮。除了这些漂亮的装饰，彩龙上还安装了精巧的机关，使龙头能喷出高高的水柱或吐出五色烟雾，龙舟在彩雾中蜿蜒前进，有如神龙降临一般。

点睛
Dotting the Eyes

龙舟装饰好后，就请一位大江冯氏男性长者给龙舟点睛。点睛者用毛笔蘸朱砂在龙眼上点几笔，同时还要口念“国泰民安”“风调雨顺”“顺风顺水”等吉利话。龙舟开眼了，就能开龙了。开龙后，龙舟要将龙头对着冯氏宗祠，三进三退磕头拜祖先，拜毕祖先，龙舟还要在风水塘中巡游三圈。旧时岸上放置有10多米高的炮架，开龙后就一直燃放炮仗，巡游结束后鞭炮屑往往数十厘米厚。在风水塘巡游时，村中富户把事先准备好的“青”（包括葱、生菜、利市、烟等），用红绳子吊在竹竿上，伸到池塘中让龙舟采，龙舟采到“青”后会三点头以示感谢，岸上也会燃放鞭炮庆祝。

大江村内有一条连接风水塘的环村涌，以前龙舟会扒到涌中巡游，往返大概10千米，再回到村中风水塘，将龙头对着冯氏世祠，三进三退磕头拜祖先，再绕风水塘巡游三圈后就可休龙了。彩龙在河涌中巡游，富裕的村民也会准备“青”，用竹竿挑着伸到河涌上，龙舟一边巡游一边采“青”，在河涌中进退摇摆，岸上鞭炮

the Fengs have invited Foshan Folk Art Society to help decorate their dragon boat. The head and the tail are made of metal, covered with waterproof fiber cloth. The boat is decorated with patterns representing Foshan culture such as the Tongji Bridge, the Ancestral Temple, Huang Feihong, Cantonese Opera characters; and patterns representing Foshan's economic development, such as Foshan New Media Industrial Park and Chanxi New Town. Apart from these beautiful and striking decorations, delicate devices are installed in the colorful dragon boat so that water columns or colored smokes can be sprayed from the dragon head. Meandering along the creeks in the colored smoke, the dragon boat looks like a divine dragon that has just descended.

After the dragon boat has been decorated, a senior male of the Fengs in Dajiang Village dots its eyes with cinnabar using a writing brush while saying some auspicious words like "prosperity for the country and peace for the people", "timely wind and rain" and "good luck". Once the eyes are "opened", the dragon boat is started. After that, the dragon boat will point its head towards the Feng Clan Ancestral Hall, kowtowing to the ancestors while moving forward and backward three times respectively. Then, the dragon boat cruises in the Fengshui Pond for three rounds. In the old days, firecracker racks of over 10 meters high were installed on the bank. After the dragon boat was started, firecrackers were set off continuously, so after the cruises, the firecracker scraps were as thick as dozens of centimeters. When the dragon boat cruises in the Fengshui Pond, some rich families tie the "greens" (including shallots, lettuces, lucky money, cigarettes, etc.) to bamboo poles with red strings and extend them to the pond for the dragon boat to catch. Once getting them, the dragon boat nods thrice to express its gratitude while firecrackers are set off on the banks.

There is a ring creek linked to the Fengshui Pond in Dajiang Village. In the past, the dragon boat would cruise in the creek, with a total distance of about 10 km. After returning to the pond, the dragon would have its head towards the Feng Clan Ancestral Hall, kowtowing to the ancestors while moving forward and backward thrice. Then it could rest after circling the pond thrice. While it was cruising in the creek, the colorful dragon boat tried to reach out to the "greens" prepared by some rich villagers, while moving forward and backward

东平河里彩龙采青
Colorful Dragon Boats Collecting the Greens in the Dongping River

and swinging to one side or another amid cheers and firecrackers, creating a festive atmosphere. Later due to industrialization and urbanization, most of the creek surrounding the village has become narrower. Moreover, some cemented bridges have been built over the creek, making it impossible to cruise and to collect the "greens" in the creek. In the past, on the sixth day of the fifth lunar month, the Fengs' colorful dragon boat of Dajiang Village would go to visit their relatives and worship their ancestors in Cuntou and Cunwei villages of Zhangcha where live large numbers of the Feng people. In recent years, the blocked creek and road construction have made it impossible to make the visit, so the ritual has stopped. When the Fengs' colorful dragon boat is cruising, there are 68 people on board, including 6 standing at the front, 6 standing at the back, 32 paddling, 2 beating the drum, 1 hitting the gong, 4 splashing water, 4 waving the flags, 6 holding the special umbrellas, 6 holding the big flags, and 1 holding the dragon card. The most important people on the colorful dragon boat are the drummers, who are responsible for directing the performances of the flaggers, the umbrella holders and the water player, for controlling the speed of the paddlers, and for directing the dragon boat to collect the greens and kowtow to the ancestors, so they must be experienced and familiar with the dragon boat rituals. The two drummers, taking the horse-riding stance, beat the drum simultaneously, first heavily on the center of the drum, then the side. The gong player just follows the rhythm of the drum. With one drumbeat followed by one gong sound, the dragon boat sets off. The six men at the bow and the stern respectively press the dragon boat rhythmically according to the direction of the drummers, so that it shakes its head or sways its tail, rises and falls while moving forward, just like a real dragon. Under the commands of the drummers, the paddlers follow the ups and

齐鸣，喝彩声不断，呈现出一片欢乐祥和的氛围。后由于工业化和城市化发展，环村涌大部分被填塞变窄，河涌上又搭建了一些低矮的水泥桥，龙舟在环村涌巡游采青的仪式再也无法进行。张槎境内的村头村、村尾村也有大量冯姓村民聚居，这些村民与大江村冯氏同宗同源，以前每逢农历五月初六，大江冯氏彩龙就会穿涌过河，游到村头村、村尾村去探亲和拜祖先。近年来，由于河涌淤塞或修路，大江彩龙无法前往村头村、村尾村，这一仪式也不再举行。

冯氏彩龙巡游时，彩龙上共有68名成员，其中龙头6人（站姿）、龙尾6人（站姿）、扒丁32人、司鼓2人、司锣1人、泼水4人、挥旗4人、扶罗伞6人、扶大旗6人、头牌1人。彩龙上的成员中最重要的就是锣鼓手，他们要指挥船上旗手、罗伞手、泼水手的表演和扒丁落扒速度，指挥龙舟采青或磕头拜祖先，因此锣鼓手必须经验丰富、熟悉龙舟礼仪。大江村的鼓手有两个，他们扎好马步，抡起鼓槌，两人同时起槌落槌，先重打鼓心数下，再敲打鼓边，锣手紧随鼓手敲锣，一声鼓一声锣，龙舟出发了。龙头、龙尾各站立6人，他们健壮有力，按照鼓手的指挥有节奏地用力摁船，使得龙舟在水中摇头摆尾、起伏前进，犹如真龙一般。扒丁在锣鼓手的指挥下，随着船身起伏划桨，落扒时疾时弛，龙舟时快时慢，有如嬉戏玩耍的孩童。罗伞手左手抓罗伞，右手执羽扇，稳住罗伞，轻摇羽扇，身体随着龙舟轻轻摆动，似闲庭信步。旗手左右舞动旗帜，两左两右，交叉变换，鲜艳的旗帜在风中飘扬，分外耀眼。在人群密集、水面宽阔处，四位泼水者趁机舀水泼出水花，时而如天女散花，时而如长龙吐水，引得观众阵阵叫好。

游龙
Dragon Boat Cruise

大江彩龙巡游表演时，会有四艘小龙舟跟随，一艘小龙舟在前面指挥，两艘小龙舟分别在彩龙左右两侧护航，还有一艘小龙舟沿途放鞭炮。负责指挥的小龙舟上通常有三人：两人负责扒龙舟，一人双手挥舞两面三角形小旗帜，配合口哨声指挥龙舟的行进方向。在小龙舟的指挥下，彩龙不断变换行进路线：直线巡游、“之”字形嬉戏、转圈表演、一进一退或三进三退向人群敬礼。看到彩龙如此精彩的表演，岸上群众的欢呼喝彩声此起彼伏，节日喜庆气氛四溢。

downs of the dragon boat, paddling sometimes rapidly and sometimes slowly, just like kids having fun. The umbrella holders hold the umbrellas steadily in their left hands and gently wave the feathered fans in their right hands while swaying slightly with the movements of the dragon boat. There are two flaggers on each side of the boat who take turns to wave the colorful flags, which make a spectacular scene. In places where there are large crowds of spectators and where the river is wide enough, the four water players seize the chance to splash water, sometimes like a celestial girl scattering flowers, sometimes like a dragon spitting water, winning cheers and applause from the audience.

When the Dajiang colorful dragon is cruising, four smaller dragon boats will keep it company, one directing in the front, two escorting by its sides, and one setting off firecrackers. There are three people on the command boat, including two paddlers and one waving two little triangular flags and blowing the whistle to guide the direction of the colorful dragon boat. Under the guidance of the command boat, the colorful dragon boat constantly changes its routes, going straight forward, zigzagging, circling, or moving forward and backward once or thrice to salute the crowds. Watching its wonderful performances, people on the banks applaud and cheer enthusiastically, creating a festive atmosphere.

4.2 Brotherly Affection of Jiujiang Dragon Boats

Since the Ming and Qing dynasties, dragon boating has been a prevalent and popular folk activity in Jiujiang, Nanhai. In the 11th year of the Zhengde period of the Ming Dynasty(1516), Zeng Chu (self-named Hai'ou Shanren), a successful candidate in the imperial examinations from Jiujiang once described in his poem of Oushan(Dandansha), "Watching dragon boat racing in the distance, seeing lone cranes from time to time." At that time, Zeng Chu, after resignation from office, was living reclusively in his hometown Oushan. On seeing the intense and wonderful dragon boat racing, he could not help going to have a look. *The Township Chronicle of Jiujiang, Nanhai* compiled by Li Chunxi and printed 1657, records, "On the Double Fifth Festival, people drink absinthe, eat Zongzi, and race dragon boats for prizes. The activities well extend to the sixth, seventh and eighth lunar months." This record shows that in the Qing Dynasty, the custom of dragon boat activities was by no means less popular than in the Ming Dynasty. *The Chronicle of Jiujiang, Town of Scholars* also makes the same reference to this festive custom. In addition, *Miscellaneous Records,* Vol. 21, of this book offers detailed descriptions of the making and decoration of dragon boats, the skills of playing the drums and gongs and waving the flags, and the enthusiasm of the spectators.

In the early years after the founding of the People's Republic of China in 1949, the dragon boat custom in Jiujiang was carried on. But due to busy farming, water levels and National Day celebrations, the dragon boat racing originally held during the Dragon Boat Festival was moved to the National Day. Around the National Day holiday each year, the mighty dragon boats shuttle in the creeks of Jiujiang Town, attracting tens of thousands of people to the riversides

第二节　九江龙舟　阿契情深

明清以来，南海九江扒龙舟活动盛行，是人民群众十分喜爱的端午民俗活动。明正德十一年（1516）中举的九江人曾储（自号海偶山人）曾在描写偶山（担担沙）的诗中云："隔岸遥看龙竞渡，半天时见鹤孤飞。"辞官回乡闲居于偶山上的曾储，看到激烈、精彩的龙舟竞渡，也不由得要去凑凑热闹。清初黎春曦纂辑的《南海九江乡志》记载："端午饮艾酒、馕角黍、竞龙舟夺标，至六七八九月，兴犹未阑。"《南海九江乡志》于顺治丁酉年（1657）刻成，此时为清初，龙舟竞渡之风仍不输于明代。光绪九年（1883）修的《九江儒林乡志》又提到了这一节俗："是月竞龙舟，或至八九月，兴犹未阑。"《九江儒林乡志》卷二十一《杂录》还对龙舟的形制与装饰，锣手、鼓手、旗手的技巧，观众的热情等进行了详细描述。

中华人民共和国成立初期，九江传统龙舟习俗得以承续。但由于农忙、水位、国庆等原因，本在端午期间举办的龙舟竞渡改在国庆举行。每年国庆前后，威武的龙舟在九江镇的河涌内穿梭往来，成千上万的人围在河涌或水塘边看龙舟，呐喊声、锣鼓声、礼炮声交织在一起，奏起了一支支激越的水乡交响曲。随着九江传统龙

九江龙舟探阿契（九江文化站）
Jiujiang Dragon Boats Visiting Sworn Brothers (Jiujiang Township Cultural Station)

舟习俗的发展，传统龙舟数量也在持续增加。2000年以后，九江新造了大量传统龙舟，截至2014年末，九江镇内共拥有传统龙舟125艘。

9月中下旬，九江人开始起龙舟，龙舟起上来后还要整修、刷油、装饰等。9月底某天的凌晨，人们划着龙舟静静前往采青地点。

龙舟食了青，精神抖擞，就要出发访阿契了。九江龙舟有结契的传统，结契就是不同村落的龙舟结为兄弟，九江几乎每条传统龙舟都有自己的阿契，目前九江镇内共有12帮阿契。九江龙舟结契既是为了有困难时互相帮助，渡过难关，也是为了在龙舟节期间营造气氛，热热闹闹赛龙舟。每年龙舟活动期间，阿契们都会互相探访，吃龙舟饭，一起出海，远征西江，展现出了九江人浓浓的人情

or the ponds. Cheers and sounds of the drums and gongs and of firecrackers are intertwined into an inspiring symphony of the water town. In recent years, with the development of traditional customs in Jiujiang, the number of dragon boats has kept increasing. Since 2000, large numbers of traditional dragon boats have been built. As of 2014, there were 125 in total in Jiujiang Town.

In mid-to-late September, the dragon boats are lifted, after which they need to be repaired or renovated, painted and decorated. On an early morning in late September, the dragon boats are rowed quietly to the place where the greens are collected.

After that, the refreshed dragon boats will set off to visit their sworn brothers. Jiujiang dragon boats have had the tradition of becoming sworn brothers with other dragon boats in nearby villages. Almost every dragon boat has a sworn brother. At present there are 12 sects of brotherhood. Such ties are formed not only to help each other in times of difficulties, but to create a festive atmosphere for dragon boat races. Every year during the dragon boat activities, all sworn brothers visit each other, have meals together, and sail to the sea and to the Xijiang River together, demonstrating great humanity and strong ties between the sworn brothers.

2012年9月16日，九江沙嘴村起龙船
Lifting the Dragon Boat in Shazui Village, Jiujiang Town on September 16th, 2012

About three to five days before the dragon boat gala, the dragon boats, decorated with the head, the tail, the drum, the gong and other ornaments, go to visit their sworn brothers in other villages. It is especially important for new dragon boats to get to know their sworn brothers. There are particular requirements for the visiting route. First, they have to visit the eldest dragon boat, then other brothers one by one along the route. At the same time they also have to visit the spiritual leaders or gods worshiped by the sworn brothers. When worshiping the spiritual leaders, all the crew go ashore bringing with them the dragon card, head, tail, drums and gongs taken from the dragon boat. Each dragon boat has to prepare its own incenses, candles and firecrackers. The dragon card must be placed in the center. The drums and gongs, lined up horizontally, are beaten fiercely to compete with each other while firecrackers are set off, rendering the occasion joyous and festive. There is also a custom of exchanging gifts when the dragon boats visit their sworn brothers. In the past, the gifts were *Gaobiao* (patterned cloth on a bamboo pole), tea and lucky money. Now they are *Gaobiao*, mineral water, fruits and lucky money.

When a visiting dragon boat comes into the creek of a village, the head of the dragon boat club of the village will lead his villagers to the riverside to salute them amid sounds of drums, gongs and firecrackers and enthusiastically invite them to have a dragon boat meal ashore. At this moment, the visiting dragon boat will thank and salute the hosts with merry rhythms of drums and gongs and cheerful shouts. Then it will row three rounds before going ashore. They will go to enjoy the dragon boat meal after sticking their visiting cards.

Every year, Jiujiang holds various dragon boat races, the largest of which is the open tournament held at the Shangdong section of the Jiujiang Creek. It is a section with a broad and straight water surface, wide banks and shaded trees, an ideal place for racing. In recent years, it attracts over 50 racing teams each year. Jiujiang Creek Open Tournament is mainly traditional straight route racing. At the sound of the starting pistol, dragon boats sprint out like arrows, accompanied by rhythmic drumbeats, cheerful shouts from the crowds and the "Hi Ho, Hi Ho" chants of the paddlers. Both banks of the Jiujiang Creek are boiling with excitement. Jiujiang, as a town famous for its dragon boat culture, has races not only for speed but also for beauty. In the beauty contests, all the dragon boats are decorated to the extreme. The head, the tail, the card, the special umbrellas, the command flags, the seven-star flags, the gong and the drum are all essential decorations of a dragon boat. Some dragon boats also use a large number of cultural elements for decorations, such as red lanterns, lions and ancient fans.

味和阿契之间的深情厚谊。

每年龙舟盛会前3~5天，戴上龙头、龙尾、锣鼓等装饰的龙舟，纷纷前往各村落探访阿契。新龙舟尤其需要访阿契，认识自己的兄弟。访阿契的路线也是有讲究的，首先要拜访契帮中的老大，然后再顺路逐个拜访各阿契，同时阿契供奉的社老或社神也要拜访。拜社老时，需要取下自己龙舟的龙牌、锣鼓、龙头、龙尾，全体人员上岸拜社老。各龙舟都自备香烛和鞭炮到贺，龙牌必须放于正中供奉，锣鼓一字排开，全力击打，但求威猛，是为斗鼓，同时鞭炮齐鸣，热闹非凡。探亲途中经过兄弟契友的村落时，还有互赠礼物的习俗，以前的礼物为高标（一根竹竿挑一块花布）、茶水、红包等，现在为高标、矿泉水、水果、红包等。

阿契送礼物
Sworn Brothers Presenting Gifts

当阿契的龙舟进入本村的河涌时，阿契龙船会负责人带领村民来到河边，向前来的龙舟拱手表示欢迎，同时锣鼓喧天、鞭炮齐鸣，热情邀请对方上岸吃龙舟饭。此时前来的龙舟用欢快的锣鼓节奏和大声呐喊向主办方表示感谢和致礼，接着龙舟还要巡游三个来回才落扒上岸，贴好龙船帖后，再去吃龙舟饭。

每年龙舟活动期间，九江都会举办大大小小的竞渡比赛，其中规模最大的要数在九江涌上东段举办的公开赛。九江涌上东段河

九江龙舟阿契出海
Jiujiang Dragon Boat Sworn Brothers Going to Sea

面宽且直，河堤宽阔，绿树成荫，是理想的竞渡地点，近年来每年都吸引了50多支队伍报名参赛。九江涌公开赛主要是传统龙舟直道竞速赛，发令枪响后，一对对龙舟如离弦之箭般冲出去，龙船鼓“咚咚咚”响着，人群中爆发出阵阵喝彩声，夹杂着扒丁们“嗨嗬，嗨嗬”的号子声，九江涌两岸都沸腾了！九江作为龙舟文化名镇，不仅有赛龙斗标，也有彩龙斗靓。斗靓时，艘艘龙舟都使出浑身解数来打扮自己，龙头、龙尾、龙牌、罗伞、帅旗、七星旗、锣、鼓等都是龙舟的必备装饰，有些龙舟还启用了大量传统元素“扮靓”，如红灯笼、醒狮、古扇等；有的龙舟还搬出了历史故事和外国名人，如草船借箭、憨豆先生、鸟叔等。

龙舟盛会落幕后，一些阿契还要结伴出海。九江龙舟出海分三派系，其出海路线和目的各不相同。六社周将军派是去下东六社拜周将军，九江有众多龙舟都和周将军上契，因此周将军派是龙舟最多的派系，也是出海规模最为壮观、最吸引人的队伍。忠山飞龙派是去担担沙——担担沙是西江中的一个岛——据说以前忠山龙舟打劫所得的财物就在担担沙分，现前往担担沙演变成为到金山寻宝，

Some others even use historical stories such as Borrowing Arrows with Thatched Boats of the Three Kingdoms or celebrities from other countries such as Mr. Bean from the UK and PSY from South Korea.

After the dragon boat gala has come to an end, some sworn brothers will go to sea together. In Jiujiang, there are three different factions of sea-going dragon boats, with different routes and purposes. The Faction of Liushe General Zhou goes to visit General Zhou in Liushe of Xiadong Village. In Jiujiang, a lot of dragon boats are sworn brothers of General Zhou, so this faction consists of the largest number of dragon boats and its sea-going scene is the most spectacular and attractive. The Faction of Zhongshan Flying Dragon goes to Dandansha, an island in the Xijiang River. It is said that in the past the Zhongshan Flying Dragon people divided what they looted from the rich at Dandansha. Nowadays, going there signifies treasure hunting and the wish for wealth. The Faction of Yuansuo Xianfeng and Waisha Liuxing, led by Xianfeng dragon boats, goes to worship Guanyin at Wanghai Guanyin Temple to pray for favorable weather and family safety. It is also said that this faction goes to sea only to visit the sworn brothers who are by the sea.

In the past, only a few dragon boats of Faction of the Liushe General Zhou went to sea. But nowadays, there are as many as 60 to 70 each year. Usually on October 2nd, after having an early lunch, people come to the creek near the

九江下西村探花桥
Tanhua (No. 3 Imperial Scholar) Bridge at Xiaxi Village, Jiujiang Town

九江乐只村望海观音庙
Wanghai Guanyin Temple at Lezhi Village, Jiujiang Town

Cimu (Tender Mother) Bridge in the old downtown area of Jiujiang at around twelve o'clock, waiting quietly for the arrival of the dragon boat Liushe General Zhou. The big crowds and incessant firecrackers further enhance the festive atmosphere. While waiting, all the dragon boats have their heads facing the Shakou Floodgate. When Liushe General Zhou arrives at the Xiahechong section at the Cimu Bridge, it will inspect the troop of dragon boats, which are lined up in accordance with their ranks. When the auspicious time comes, the drums and gongs are sounding together and firecrackers set off. Led by Liushe General Zhou, the dragon boats set off to Shakou Floodgate, which slowly opens. When each dragon boat comes near the floodgate, it is given a command flag which has been consecrated in the General Temple. It is a little triangular red flag with the Chinese character of "command" on it to bless the boat a smooth and safe journey. All the dragon boats have their club flags fixed at the heads. It is such a fascinating scene that all the paddlers are rowing fiercely and the dozens of dragon boats rushing through the floodgate, while all the drums and gongs are being played loudly and the spectators are swarming and shouting on both sides of the river.

After passing the floodgate in batches, the dragon boats turn left and proceed downstream. With strong winds and big waves in the Xijiang River, the dragon boats can be easily overturned, so the paddlers have to row hard to stabilize their boats. In the vicinity of the General Zhou Temple at Xiadong, a dragon gate made of bamboo is installed over the river. On the gate are eye-catching flags in red, yellow and green. Led by Liushe General Zhou, all the dragon boats go through the gate one by one. After that they turn

出海龙舟到达铜鼓滩水域
Dragon Boats Setting off to Sea and Reaching Tonggu Waters

寓意财源广进，大发大旺。圆所先锋、外沙六姓派出海由先锋打头阵，领头出海，是去望海观音庙拜望海观音，祈求风调雨顺、阖家平安；另有一说是圆所先锋、外沙六姓派出海是因为外沙六姓和月田圣帝两契友在海边，出海只是去探访这两个契友。

早些年，六社周将军派出海只有几条船跟随，到现在每年出海都有六七十艘龙舟。一般10月2日中午，大家都早早地吃完龙舟饭，12点左右，就来到九江旧城区慈母桥附近河涌，静待六社周将军的到来。河岸两边人头攒动，沿途不断有市民燃放鞭炮，喜庆的氛围更加浓烈。等待期间，所有龙舟都会将龙头对着沙口水闸的方向。六社周将军来到慈母桥下河涌段后，首先会检阅一下这支队伍，所有龙舟会按照辈分高低排好次序。吉时一到，锣鼓齐鸣，数十艘龙舟在六社周将军领头下，一艘紧跟一艘向沙口水闸进发。在锣鼓喧腾和鞭炮齐鸣声中，水闸门徐徐开启。临近沙口水闸，有专人向各龙舟发放由大将庙开光的令旗（写了一个“令”字的小三角红旗，保佑出海顺利平安）。龙舟上的人们将令旗插在龙头上，扒丁便纷纷用力划桨，努力冲出水闸，此时所有龙舟鼓手都会大力擂鼓，几十面龙船鼓一起奏响，震耳欲聋的鼓声、向前疾驰的数十艘龙舟、两岸汹涌的人潮，其场景非常震撼。

龙舟分批过了水闸之后，左拐弯向下游方向进发。西江风大浪大，稍有不慎，龙舟就有可能翻沉，因此扒丁都要拼命划船，稳住龙舟。扒到下东水域周将军庙附近，靠近江边有一个用竹子搭建的龙门，龙门上插着红、黄、绿三色彩旗，非常显眼。还是由六社周将军领头穿过龙门，其他龙舟一艘艘排着队穿越龙门。龙舟穿过龙门后就掉头，向岸边扒，接过岸上人递过来的彩旗，然后在附近休息或互相泼水嬉戏。一直等到所有龙舟都穿越龙门接过彩旗以后，便一起按原路返回。

龙舟盛会结束后，访阿契的龙舟马上要踏上回程，主家则要开始“送阿契”。以前送阿契的时候，主人把阿契送出村中河涌之后，阿契又回过头送回主人。一来一往，来回相送，迟迟不肯回程，这种来回相送会一直持续到次日天亮才以主人将船体打横以阻止客人继续相送而结束。

九江上东村的送阿契仪式最为隆重，后来又不断加入新的元素，逐渐演变为现在的龙舟夜游活动。当天晚上，河道两岸张灯结彩，灿烂的烟花将夜空照得如同白昼，两岸聚集了无数热情的村民，龙舟夜游过程中，一直燃放鞭炮，船上敲锣打鼓，热闹非凡。一直到晚上十点多，龙舟夜游才渐至尾声。按照传统，主人家把龙舟横在九江涌，把桨定住，才能拦住热情的阿契，劝他们不要再继续相送。阿契们只好挥桨一一道别，相约来年再见。

around and row to the bank. Having taken the colorful flags passed to them, they either took a rest in the surroundings or splashed water at each other for fun. It is after all the dragon boats have finished the ritual that they return in the same route.

After the dragon boat gala, the visiting dragon boats are to start their return trip and the hosts start "seeing off the sworn brothers". In the past, after the hosts saw the sworn brothers out of the village creek, the latter accompanied the former back to the village. They went back and forth again and again, unwilling to part with each other. It lasted until the early next morning when the hosts finally blocked the waterway with their dragon boats to prevent the guests from coming back again.

Shangdong Village of Jiujiang has the grandest ceremony of seeing off their sworn brothers, which, with the addition of new elements, has gradually become a night cruise. On the very night, the river banks are illuminated by lights and colorful decorations and the sky is turned as bright as in the daytime by brilliant fireworks. Numerous villagers gather on both sides of the river, watching the night cruise of the dragon boats amid the incessant sounds of firecrackers, drums and gongs. The night cruise does not end until after 10 p.m. According to tradition, the hosts would lay their dragon boats horizontally in the river and hold them steady with the paddles to prevent their enthusiastic sworn brothers from coming back again. So the latter wave goodbye with their paddles and promise to see each other in the coming year.

4.3 Centuries-old Yanbu Old Dragon Ritual

The Yanbu Old Dragon ritual originated from a dragon boat race in the Pearl River over 400 years ago. Since the ancient times, the Pearl River has been the most important site of dragon boat racing in Guangzhou, Dragon boats from Guangzhou and other places of Guangdong Province compete with each other fiercely there. Wang Shizhen, a famous poet in the early Qing Dynasty described the competing scenes vividly in his poem *Canton Zhuzhici* (a style of poem developed from ancient folk songs).

Legend has it that in 1597, the 25th year of the Wanli period of the Ming Dynasty, over one hundred powerful dragon boats from Nanhai County competed with each other in the Pearl River. After racing fiercely for several hours on end, Yanbu Old Dragon Boat and Pantang Dragon Boat were to compete for the championship when the spectators crowding the banks were cheering thunderously. Near the finishing line, Yanbu Old Dragon Boat was ahead of Pantang Dragon Boat by half a head. Seeing that the former was winning, a man at the head of the latter jumped into the water and snatched the target flag. Pantang won and got the flag and a roast pig. After knowing the details, the elders of Pantang thought its dragon boat had violated the rules of the competition and that the champion ship should have belonged to Yanbu Old Dragon Boat, so they had the roast pig and flag sent back to Yanbu. However, Yanbu would not accept them, which were sent back and forth several times. Seeing that the pig was getting stale but the problem was not yet solved, an elder from Pantang suggested, "Since the two sides are so sincere and courteous, let the two places be father and son and be good to each other." His suggestion won the consensus from people of the two places, so according to the time when the

第三节　盐步老龙礼俗　礼义百年传承

盐步老龙礼俗，源于400多年前珠江河上的一次龙舟竞渡。自古以来，珠江就是广州龙舟竞渡最重要的场地，不仅有广州龙舟参与，还有广东各地龙舟前来赛龙。全省精锐龙舟共聚比赛，赛事自是无比激烈。清初著名诗人王士祯的《广州竹枝词》将这种激烈的比赛场景描画得非常生动："潮来濠畔接江波，鱼藻门边净绮罗。两岸画栏红照水，疍船齐唱木鱼歌。""海珠石上柳荫浓，队队龙舟出浪中。一抹斜阳照金碧，齐将孔翠作船篷。"

相传在明万历二十五年（1597），南海县上百艘龙舟聚集在珠江河上竞渡夺标。那时南海水乡的龙舟，艘艘都很生猛。经过数个小时的激烈竞赛，最后就由盐步老龙和泮塘龙舟争夺冠军，两边河岸站满了观众，呐喊助威的声音响彻云霄。临近终点时，盐步老龙比泮塘龙舟快半个龙船头的位置，眼看盐步老龙就要夺得冠军了，不料泮塘龙舟龙头的人突然一个鱼跃扎进水中，夺了标旗，随后以冠军名义领了锦旗和烧猪。泮塘龙舟回家后，泮塘父老得知了夺标实情，认为泮塘龙舟坏了比赛规矩，冠军应该属于盐步老龙，于是派人将烧猪、锦旗送回盐步，盐步人却不肯收下，双方推来推去，眼看烧猪都要臭了，事情还没有解决。此时，有泮塘父老进言：“既然双方真诚礼让，倒不如两地结拜为父子，长年相敬。”建议得到了两地民众的一致同意，于是根据两条龙舟所造时间之先后、历史之长短划分辈分，泮塘龙舟为“契仔”（干儿子），盐步老龙被推为“契爷”（干爹），并择日簪花挂红，举行了隆重的结拜仪式。

据传明代有陶姓驸马到珠江犒龙舟，目睹盐步老龙和泮塘龙舟如此威猛，亦闻盐步老龙与泮塘龙舟结拜之事，就授意把盐步老龙、泮塘凸眼龙、白沙红龙、雅瑶东涌龙、石井古料大头龙等五艘龙舟定为“五经魁”(“经”指儒家五经《诗经》《尚书》《周易》《礼记》《春秋》)。这五条船均为快船，其龙牌为白底黑字，一直沿用至今。又传慈禧太后得知赛龙结契之事后，便赐给盐步龙舟“盐步老龙”之称，并赐十二支“雉鸡尾”、一个孖金钱、一面百足旗；赐给泮塘龙舟九支“雉鸡尾”，一个孖金钱。从此盐

12支雉鸡尾，下部为孖金钱（大沥镇文化站）
12 Pheasant Feathers with a Twin Coin at the Bottom (Dali Township Cultural Station)

百足旗（大沥镇文化站）
The Long Flag (Dali Township Cultural Station)

盐步老龙
Yanbu Old Dragon

two dragon boats were built, the Pantang Dragon Boat became an "adopted son" of Yanbu Old Dragon Boat. The two places held a grand ceremony of bonding on some auspicious day.

It is said that an emperor's son-in-law with the surname Tao in the Ming Dynasty went to reward the dragon boats in the Pearl River one day. Seeing the powerful Yanbu Old Dragon Boat and Pantang Dragon Boat, and hearing the story of their bonding, he designated the five dragon boats, namely, Yanbu Old Dragon, Pantang Bulging-Eye Dragon, Baisha Red Dragon, Yayao Dongchong Dragon and Shijing Guliao Big Head Dragon the "Top Five Dragon Boats", all of which are fast boats. Their dragon cards are white with black Chinese characters, which have been in use to this day. It is also said that after Empress Dowager Cixi heard of the story of the two dragon boats, she bestowed the title "Yanbu Old Dragon", twelve "pheasant feathers", a twin-coin, and a long flag on the Yanbu dragon boat; and nine "pheasant feathers" and a twin-coin on the

Pantang dragon boat. From then on, Yanbu Old Dragon has become a senior and no longer taken part in dragon boat races but cruises. Since Yanbu Old Dragon and Pantang young dragon have established the adoption relationship, on the fifth day of the fifth lunar month of each year, the "adopted father" will go from Yanbu, Nanhai to Pantang to visit his "adopted son". On the next day, the latter will pay the former a return visit at Yanbu. This tradition of mutual visits has been kept over the past four centuries.

Before the first day of the fifth lunar month comes, a dragon lifting ceremony will be held for Yanbu Old Dragon, which takes place at an auspicious time on an auspicious day. The elders lead the paddlers to the side of the Old Dragon bed (the Longchong River). They worship the Old Dragon with paper horses, spells, apples, peanuts, roast pigs, and other sacrificial items, while burning incenses and candles and setting off firecrackers. After the worshiping ceremony is completed, the paddlers jump into the river to lift the dragon boat, which will then be cleaned with water and polished with lard or fat pork. The Old Dragon has to finish collecting the greens before worshiping at the Huaguang Temple on the first day of the fifth lunar month.

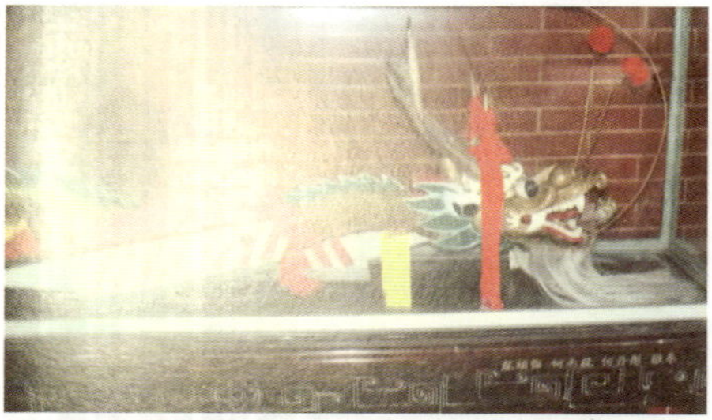

盐步老龙拜华光

Yanbu Old Dragon Worshiping the Huaguang Temple

On the first day of the fifth lunar month, the Old Dragon Boat goes to the Huaguang Temple to

步老龙成为长者，不再参加龙舟比赛，只参加游龙活动。自盐步老龙与泮塘小龙结契之后，每年五月初五，“契爷”从南海盐步去泮塘探望“契仔”。五月初六，泮塘“契仔”又来盐步探问“契爷”。400多年来，盐步老龙与泮塘契仔间的“父子”互访礼俗一直在传承。

每年农历五月朔日之前，盐步老龙就要举行起龙仪式。起龙要择定吉日吉时，由村中长老带领扒丁们来到老龙龙床边（龙涌河）祭龙。人们准备了纸马、符箓、生果（花生、苹果）、烧猪等祭品，同时燃烧香烛，放鞭炮，祭拜老龙。祭龙仪式完成后，扒丁们纷纷跳入河涌中起龙舟，龙舟起上来后，再将老龙清洗干净，并用猪油或肥猪肉擦拭船身。最迟在五月初一拜华光庙之前，老龙就要完成采青。

每年农历五月初一，盐步老龙要去华光庙拜华光大帝。华光大帝为道教神灵，又是司火之神，故忌火的粤剧艺人、冶铁工人、烧陶工人等都祭祀华光大帝。白天，村民们将老龙扒到华光庙埠头，扒丁拆下龙头、龙尾，龙头在前，龙尾在后，十三响铜锣开道，在众人的簇拥之下前往华光庙。扒丁带着龙头、龙尾来到华光庙后，摆上生果、烧猪，由仪式主持者焚香，率众人一起祭拜。老龙龙头、龙尾平时也是存放在华光庙中供人瞻仰。

祭拜完华光大帝，龙头、龙尾归位，老龙继续游三河，即游盐步大涌、河西涌、河东涌——盐步老龙由河中、河东、河西三河乡人共同制造，老龙每年都要在三河乡的河涌中巡游一遍，为大家祈福。每当隐隐约约的锣鼓声传来，村民们就会快速聚集到河涌边，

五月初五盐步老龙泮塘省亲，泮塘长老为老龙“簪花挂红”（大沥镇文化站）
Pantang Elders Hanging Flowers and Red Ribbons for Yanbu Old Dragon during its Visit to Pantang on the Fifth Day of the Fifth Lunar Month (Dali Township Cultural Station)

占据有利位置，争睹老龙风采。老龙龙标（先行船、引路船）携带拜帖，送给在河涌边等待的各村社或龙船会负责人，他们接受拜帖后，就回赠利市和礼物。

每年农历五月初五，“契爷”盐步老龙前往泮塘探“契仔”。当天一大早，泮塘人扶老携幼前往村前河涌边，等待迎接老龙，希望得到老龙的祝福，醒狮队伍也会到现场助兴。泮塘仁威、四约、五约三条龙舟在花地河（现为山村桥附近）上依次排开，恭候老龙，村里还派出“龙标”到花地河迎接老龙。

盐步老龙一进入泮塘水域，两岸群众骚动起来，鞭炮齐鸣、锣鼓喧天、醒狮腾挪跳跃，河中等待的龙舟鼓手们拼命擂鼓，用高

worship Emperor Huaguang, who is a Taoist deity and a fire god and is therefore worshiped by people who should be cautious about fire such as Cantonese Opera artists, iron smelters, and pottery workers. During the daytime, after rowing the Old Dragon to the quay of the Huaguang Temple, the paddlers take off the dragon head and the tail and carry them along, with the head in front followed by the tail. Accompanied by 13 sounds of drums and gongs, they go to the Huaguang Temple. Then they present apples, peanuts, and roast pigs and worship the Emperor together led by the host of ceremony who burns the incenses and candles. In the non-racing seasons, the Old Dragon's head and tail are stored in this temple for people to worship.

After worshiping Emperor Huaguang, the dragon head and tail are reassembled. Then the Old Dragon continues to cruise the three rivers of Yanbu Creek, Hexi Creek and Hedong Creek. Because Yanbu Old Dragon Boat was jointly built by the three villages of Hezhong, Hedong and Hexi, it will cruise the river areas of these villages each year to wish them good luck and happiness. On hearing the sounds of drums and gongs in the distance, the villagers will rush out to the riverside and occupy some advantageous location to watch the Old Dragon. The leading boat and the guide boat of the Old Dragon will present the visiting cards to the heads of different village communities or dragon boat clubs who are waiting by the river. After accepting the cards, they return their kindness with lucky money and gifts.

On the fifth day of the fifth lunar month, the "adopted father" Yanbu Old Dragon goes to visit his "adopted sons" at Pantang. Early in the morning, the Pantang people, old and young, go to the riverside to welcome the Old Dragon and to receive its blessings. There are also lion dances to boost the atmosphere. The three dragon boats of Pantang called Renwei, Siyue and Wuyue, as well as laeding boats and guide boats are waiting on the Huadi River (near the Shancun Bridge) for the Old Dragon.

Once Yanbu Old Dragon enters the Pantang waters, it is received with the greatest enthusiasm, with the spectators on both banks shouting cheerfully, firecrackers being set off, the drums and gongs sounding loudly, and the lions jumping and tumbling. Even if other dragon boats may have arrived earlier than

五月初五盐步老龙泮塘省亲父子龙船“游龙”（大沥镇文化站）

Cruise of Yanbu Old Dragon and its Adopted Sons in Pantang on the Fifth Day of the Fifth Lunar Month (Dali Township Cultural Station)

the Old Dragon, they have to wait for it to pass through the floodgate first. Then the floodgate is lifted to let in water to irrigate the fields. It is said that the Old Dragon Boat water is conducive to the proliferation of humans and animals of Pantang. As soon as they see the "adopted father", dozens of village elders who have been waiting at the pier for long, wave their hands and salute, saying some auspicious words to show their respect. When the Old Dragon comes to the Pantang pier, old people, women and children all surround it, stroking its beard, head and body, to pray for good health and good luck. Two of the elders come to the Old Dragon, putting red silk and golden flowers on its horns. They also present it with a pair of black satin banners, with words telling its laudable stories in winning the races and establishing the bond. In addition, it is also given the five beauties (five typical local produces of Pantang), good wine and lucky money, and a roast pig in years with good harvests to show their filial piety. After accepting the gifts, the Old Dragon will present its "adopted sons" with the dragon boat invitations for the "Dragon Boat Gala" at Yanbu the next day.

After the ceremony of presenting the dragon boat invitations, drums and gongs are beaten violently to signify the start of the next activity, that is, the father and sons cruising and playing together. Renwei is leading in front while Siyue and

亢密集的鼓声欢迎“契爷”。即使有其他龙舟先到，也必须等老龙先入闸。有人去打开窦闸、水口，放水灌田，据说老龙龙船水有助泮塘人畜兴旺的奇效。埠头上早有数十位泮塘父老等候多时，他们一看到“契爷”，就挥手致意，行拱手礼，口中说着吉利话。老龙来到泮塘埠头，老人、妇女、小孩纷纷上前围住老龙，抚摸老龙龙须、龙头、龙身，据传这样能使人身体康健、无灾无病。等候的两位长老走到老龙跟前，为老龙“簪花挂红”，将红绸金花挂在老龙龙角上。两位长老还将一对黑纱绸锦旗赠给老龙，上书“昔日夺标同鼎甲，当年沧海占群龙”和“昔日夺标同结契，当年沧海冠群龙”。泮塘还会送上“泮塘五秀”、美酒和利市等，遇上好年成还会送一只烧猪孝敬“契爷”。老龙收下礼物后会向“契仔”送上龙船帖，邀请泮塘龙舟参与盐步五月初六的“龙船景”。

送完龙船帖，水上立刻锣鼓喧天，进入契爷、契仔结伴游龙戏水环节（盐步、泮塘人称之为“操水”）。游龙时，仁威龙舟开路，四约、五约龙舟陪伴老龙。按照传统的做法，父子游龙至少要往返三个来回。船头、船尾各站立几人，他们同时发力，身体有韵律地蹬船，其他扒丁同时用力扒船，龙船犹如一条真龙在水中摇头摆尾，快速前进。泮塘友好村、兄弟村等邻村龙舟跟随其后，一同参与“游龙”。

迎接完“契爷”后，好客的泮塘人总要大开筵席，款待亲朋。盐步老龙队伍入座主位，与众人共享美味又“好意头”的龙船饭。饭后“契仔”依依不舍地送别“契爷”，直到闸口（花地河段）才举手揖别。

五月初六，泮溏龙舟回访“契爷”盐步老龙。这天一大早，老龙一身盛装，印有“盐步老龙”四个大字的百足旗迎风飘扬，威风凛凛，驶进聚龙河段（过去是石潭口）兴奋地等待“契仔”。河岸上站满了想一睹“契爷”“契仔”相会盛景的人群。

伴随泮塘龙舟前来探亲的队伍中有茶滘、坑口等地的龙舟，各龙舟到达盐步大闸前集队等候。其间各龙舟一直敲锣打鼓，岸上鞭炮齐鸣，人们欢呼问候不断，热闹非凡。等全部龙舟到位后，由泮塘龙舟大声擂鼓，率领进闸。

龙舟队伍浩浩荡荡进闸后，“契爷”开始给“契仔”回礼，包括盐步秋茄、白酒以及象征友谊的黑纱绸标旗，标旗上书“永结交情知此日，幸同夺锦忆当年”和“不断交情知此日，幸同结契忆当年”。“契爷”领头，泮塘龙舟紧随其后，其他龙舟尾随，一字形朝前进发。沿途鞭炮齐鸣，乡人纷纷欢迎“契仔”等贵宾。龙舟队伍一路前行到华光庙和龙涌河，分别祭拜华光大帝和老龙龙床，并在龙涌、华光庙埗头之间往返巡游三次以结束参拜。参拜后开始吃龙舟饭。

每年五月初六，盐步各自然村及邻近地区的龙舟汇集盐步河上，举行锦龙盛会。上午各地龙舟到达后，就在盐步河上游龙，数百艘龙舟在河面上巡游，彩旗招展，锣鼓喧天，岸边人潮涌动，好不热闹。热情慈祥的盐步老龙一直在河面上巡游，欢迎各地龙舟来到盐步做客，长长的白髯在风中飘拂。吃过龙舟饭，就开始赛龙，一般要经过初赛、复赛、决赛三轮比赛，决出前三名。赛龙时，盐步老龙和泮塘龙舟都不参加比赛。自20世纪80年

Wuyue are on both sides of the Old Dragon. According to traditional practices, they have to cruise at least three rounds. Several people stand on the bow and stern respectively, pressing the boats rhythmically, while the paddlers row with all their might, so the dragon boats are just like real dragons, nodding their heads and swaying their tails while moving forward rapidly. Dragon boats from friendly and brother villages of Pantang also join in the cruise by following the Old Dragon.

After welcoming the "adopted father", the hospitable Pantang people always hold a grand banquet to entertain friends and relatives. The Yanbu Old Dragon people take the most important seats, enjoying the delicious and auspicious dragon boat meal with everyone. After the meal, the "adopted sons" bid farewell to the "adopted father" reluctantly at the floodgate.

On the next day, Pantang dragon boats pay a return visit to Yanbu Old Dragon, the "adopted father". Early in the morning, the Old Dragon, fully dressed up with the long flag writing "Yanbu Old Dragon" fluttering in the wind, is waiting for the "adopted sons" excitedly in the Julong (Dragon-gathering) Section. The banks are crowded with people eager to watch the grand meeting between the "adopted father and sons".

Coming together with the Pantang dragon boats are dragon boats from Chajiao, Kengkou and other places, all of which wait at the floodgate of Yanbu. During this time, drums and gongs are beaten continuously and firecrackers set off while people are shouting and greeting each other enthusiastically. When all the dragon boats are in

五月初五盐步老龙泮塘省亲享受传统大盆菜（大沥镇文化站）

Traditional Big Pot Dish during Yanbu Old Dragon's Visit at Pantang on the Fifth Day of the Fifth Lunar Month (Dali Township Cultural Station)

place, the Pantang dragon boats will beat the drums and lead them to pass the floodgate.

After all the dragon boats have entered the floodgate, the "adopted father" starts giving the "adopted sons" gifts in return, including Yanbu eggplants, liquor and a pair of black silk banners symbolizing friendship on which words recalling their centuries-old bond are written. With Yanbu Old Dragon taking the lead, followed by Pantang dragon boats and then others, they proceed one by one. The villagers welcome the distinguished guests from Guangzhou with firecrackers being set off along the way. When the team arrives at the Huaguang Temple and the Longchong River, they worship Emperor Huaguang and the Old Dragon Bed and cruise three rounds between Longchong and the Huaguang Temple pier. After that, they start enjoying the dragon boat meal.

On the sixth day of the fifth lunar month each year, a grand dragon boat gala is held in the Yanbu River, with dragon boats of the natural villages in Yanbu and nearby regions taking part. In the morning after several hundred dragon boats from different places have arrived, they cruise the river, amid sounds of drums and gongs, and cheers and shouts of the people. The enthusiastic and kind Old Dragon is cruising and welcoming its guests from different places, its white beard swaying in the wind. The dragon boat racing starts after the meal, including a preliminary, semi-final and a final to delermine the first three places. Yanbu Old Dragon and Pantang dragon boats do not take part in the race. Since the 1980s, Pantang has organized hundreds of villagers to watch the grand dragon boat gala at Yanbu each year, who have been warmly received by the Yanbu people.

The race is followed by a dragon boat cruise performance. The Old Dragon takes the lead, followed by its "adopted sons" Pantang dragon boats and escorted by others. They cruise three rounds before ending the performance. After that, other dragon boats leave one by one, but the "adopted father and sons" continue to play on water. It is not until the sun has set that Yanbu Old Dragon will bid farewell to Pantang dragon boats. They go side by side in and out of the Yanbu waterway thrice before parting with each other.

For the past several hundred years, no matter how the natural and social environments have changed, the people of Yanbu and Pantang, with the dragon

五月初六盐步老龙盐步涌上展示的全部行头（大沥镇文化站）
Outfits of Yanbu Old Dragon in the Yanbu Creek on the Sixth Day of the Fifth Lunar Month (Dali Township Cultural Station)

代开始，泮塘每年都组织数百乡亲来盐步欣赏锦龙盛会，受到盐步人的热情接待。

赛龙结束后，是“契爷”“契仔”的游龙表演。各龙舟抖擞精神，盐步老龙领头，泮塘龙舟紧随“契爷”左右，形影不离，其他龙舟护航，龙舟队共做三个来回折返后结束游玩活动。之后，其他龙舟陆续离开，“契爷”“契仔”继续在河面上游龙戏水。直到太阳偏西，盐步老龙才送别泮塘龙舟，它们并肩而行，三进三出盐步水道，一直送至聚龙（过去是石潭口）甚至东漖河段，才拱手作别。

数百年来，不管自然环境、社会环境如何变化，盐步与泮塘两地人民以龙舟为媒介，一直保持着友情和交往。同时盐步老龙因与泮塘龙舟的关系，与茶滘、坑口等地的龙船也结为朋友。盐步老龙早已超越了村落氏族的标志，成为仁义、孝悌、友善、谦虚等传统文化的传播者和友谊使者，促进了盐步、泮塘两地以及广佛接壤之地的和谐相处与共同发展。

boats as a medium, have maintained their friendship and communication. Because of its relationship with Pantang dragon boats, Yanbu Old Dragon Boat has made friends with dragon boats of Chajiao, Kengkou and other places. Yanbu Old Dragon has become more than a symbol of villages and clans, but a disseminator of the traditional culture such as benevolence, filial piety, friendliness, and modesty and also a messenger of friendship, promoting the harmonious coexistence and common development of Yanbu and Pantang as well as other adjacent areas of Guangzhou and Foshan.

4.4 Dragon Sons Visiting Huangqi Dragon Mother Temple

Huangqi is a water village with a densely distributed water network. It used to be called Huangzhuqi Town and Huangzhuqi Village before the founding of the People's Republic of China. The Pearl River and its tributaries including the Yayao Waterway and the Baisha River, together with several dozen creeks, either run by or through the village, which leads to the popularity of water god worship. The Dragon Mother is the most important water deity in Huangqi and a very important one in the Pearl River Delta.

Nanyue Chronicle by Liu Xun of the Tang Dynasty, *Taiping Huanyu Ji (General Geography of China)* by Le Shi of the early Song Dynasty, *New Notes on Guangdong* by Qu Dajun of the late Ming and early Qing dynasties, and *News in Canton* by Fan Duan'ang of the Qing Dynasty all have records of the Dragon Mother, of which those by Qu Dajun are the most detailed.

> The Dragon Mother, Lady Wen was from Chengshui, Jinkang. Qin Shihuang, First Emperor of Qin once wanted to make her a concubine but she was reluctant. The messenger urged her to start the voyage. When the boat arrived in Shi'an, a dragon led the boat carrying her back to Chengshui. This process was repeated several times. After Lady Wen died she was buried on Xiyuan, where the dragon tried to create big waves to turn sand into a tomb for her. Later big wind and heavy rain moved the tomb to the north of the river. Whenever the tomb is submerged in flood, though the surroundings are muddy, the water a few feet around the tomb is always clear. There are mountains to the south of the tomb. Before rain, clouds come out from the mountains, which are shaded by ancient trees several hundred years old. Nobody dares to chop down the trees because they believe that the spirit

第四节 黄岐龙母庙 龙子参拜忙

黄岐是一个岭南水乡村落，中华人民共和国成立前有黄竹岐堡、黄竹岐乡之称，中华人民共和国成立后称为黄岐。其境内水道河涌密布，珠江、珠江支流雅瑶水道、白沙河，或在村边奔涌，或穿村而过，还有数十条较小的河涌像毛细血管一般分布于黄岐村。水网纵横、河涌密布的环境，使得黄岐的水神崇拜之风兴盛。龙母是黄岐最重要的水神，也是珠三角地区重要的水神。

唐刘恂的《南越志》、宋初乐史的《太平寰宇记》、明末清初屈大均的《广东新语》、清范端昂的《粤中见闻》都有关于龙母的记载，其中以屈大均的记载最为详细。

> 龙母温夫人者，晋康程水人也。秦始皇尝遣使尽礼致聘，将纳夫人后宫，夫人不乐。使者敦迫上道，行至始安，一夕龙引所乘船还程水，使者复往，龙复引船以归。夫人没，葬西源上，龙尝为大波，萦浪转沙以成坟，会大风雨，墓移江北，每洪水淹没，四周皆浊，而近墓数尺独清。墓之南有山，天将雨，云气必先群山而出，树林阴（荫）翳，有数百年古木，人不敢伐，以夫人有神灵其间云。夫人姓蒲，误作温，然其墓当灵溪水口，灵溪一名温水，以夫人姓温故名。或曰，温者，媪

之讹也。夫人故称蒲媪，又称媪龙。唐李绅诗：风水多虞祝媪龙。然媪非生龙者也。得大卵而蓄之，龙子出焉。养之以饮食物，龙得长大，盖古之豢龙氏也。始皇以为神，遣使迎媪。以尝闻徐福言，海神之使者铜色而龙形，光上照天，意媪其同类也，求三神山患且至，船风辄引而去，岂亦龙之所为耶。

由记载可知龙母为今德庆悦城人士，因拾龙卵蓄之，并豢养龙长大，成为龙母，乡人以神视之。

后来各朝均很重视龙母，对龙母封赐有加，甚至由道教“三天上帝”册封其为“水府元君”，显示出这位龙母由人变为水神。农历五月初八是其诞日，香火鼎盛。龙母崇拜遍布于西江流域，中华人民共和国成立前有龙母庙数千，目前尚有大小龙母庙数百。其中以德庆悦城龙母祖庙最为著名，相传德庆悦城为龙母故乡，这座规模宏大的庙宇始建于秦汉，历代均有修葺，至今已有两千多年历史。每逢农历五月初八龙母诞期，龙母祖庙都举行大规模的民间祭祀活动，肇庆市属各县及珠江三角洲，甚至港澳地区都有民众去参拜，多时超过十万之众，最少也有数万人。一连十数日，龙母祖庙前的石牌坊广场上，信众云集，香烟缭绕。

信众为龙母祝寿
Disciples Celebrating the Dragon Mother's Birthday

> of the lady is in there. The lady's surname was Pu, which was mistaken as Wen. Her tomb is at the mouth of the Lingxi River, which is also called Wen Water, named after the lady's surname. Another legend has it that Wen is a mistaken sound of Ao, which means an old lady, so the lady is also called Pu'ao, or Ao Dragon. Li Shen of the Tang Dynasty wrote the verse, "Fengshui blesses the Ao dragon". However, Ao did not give birth to the dragon. She once got a big egg and kept it, and the dragon was hatched and then grew up. Qin Shihuang thought her a deity and tried to marry her, who was believed to be of the same kind of dragon-shaped sea deity with bronze skin.

The records reveal that the Dragon Mother was from Yuecheng, Deqing, Guangdong Province. Because she picked up a dragon egg and kept it, and raised the dragon, she was called the Dragon Mother and regarded a deity by the villagers.

Later dynasties all attached great importance to the Dragon Mother and awarded her various titles. The Emperor of Three Heavens of Taoism even bestowed on her the title "Monarch of the Water Temple", indicating that she was transformed from a human being into a water deity. On her birthday on the eighth day of the fifth lunar month, she is worshiped by numerous disciples. The Dragon Mother worship was prevalent in the Xijiang River valley, where there were thousands of Dragon Mother temples before the founding of the People's Republic of China in

龙母胜迹
Dragon Mother Scenery

1949. Now, there are still hundreds of them left, among which Yuecheng Dragon Mother Ancient Temple in her legendary hometown Deqing is the most famous. The temple was first built during the Qin and Han dynasties with a history of over 2,000 years and has been renovated for numerous times. On her birthday, large-scale folk worshiping activities are held at the Dragon Mother Ancient Temple, which attract people from different counties of Zhaoqing City, from the Pearl River Delta, and even from Hong Kong and Macao. The numbers range from tens of thousands to hundreds of thousands. For more than ten days on end, the square in front of the temple is crowded with disciples and covered with smokes from burning incenses and candles.

There are two legends about the origin of Huangqi Dragon Mother. One is that during the Wanli period (1573-1619) of the Ming Dynasty, the Xijiang River valley was flooded. The turbulent water submerged most parts of Nanhai and Shunde in the lower reaches of the Xijiang River for half a month without any sign of retreat. One morning, an old woman from Huangzhuqi went to the river and found that the water had retreated a lot. She found elatedly a carved wooden statue of the Dragon Mother on the bank. The old woman cleaned it and placed it where the people boarded the ferry. Whenever the villagers suffered from some diseases or disasters, they went to pray in front of the Dragon Mother statue and it often worked. Therefore, more and more people went to worship her. Later the villagers built a Dragon Mother Temple there to bless people in the surroundings.

Another legend says that during the Wanli period of the Ming Dynasty, several senior disciples of Huangzhuqi went to the Dragon Mother Temple in Deqing and stayed in Yuecheng for a night. All of them had the same dream in which the Dragon Mother told them, "From now on, you don't have to come all the way here. Go and build a temple in your place." Greatly startled, the disciples went to tell the attendant of the Dragon Mother Ancient Temple in Yuecheng, Deqing about their dreams and the attendant said he also had the same dream. Therefore, the disciples escorted a wooden statue of the Dragon Mother from Yuecheng to Huangzhuqi.

According to *Nanhai County Chronicle* which was compiled in the 15th year of

关于黄岐龙母的来历有两种传说。一说明万历年间（1573—1620），西江流域发大水，汹涌的江水奔涌而下，西江下游的南海、顺德等地大部分被水淹了，大水半个月未退。一天上午，南海黄竹岐有位老妇人到江边看水势，发现水退了不少，满心欢喜时在岸边发现了一尊龙母木雕像。老妇人便将龙母像清洗干净，将其安置在渡口处。每当乡民有什么病痛灾难，就去渡口龙母像前祭拜祈祷，时有灵验。由是渡口龙母像前香火日隆，村民遂在渡口建立了一座龙母庙，护佑四方百姓。

又一说在明朝万历年间，黄竹岐几个年长信徒到德庆龙母庙参拜，在悦城住了一晚，众人晚间做了一个相同的梦，梦中龙母对他们说，以后你们不用再远来了，就在你们当地立庙祭拜吧。信众很惊奇，就一同去找德庆悦城龙母祖庙的庙祝说他们的梦境，庙祝说他也做了一个一样的梦。于是，信徒便将德庆悦城龙母庙的一个龙母木雕神像请到了黄竹岐。

明万历年间，黄竹岐乡人便在江边供奉龙母神像，后来还修建了龙母庙。清道光十五年（1835）修、清同治十一年（1872）刻的《南海县志》记载了龙母庙的位置“在黄竹岐乡东北”，可见在明万历年间至清道光十五年之间，黄竹岐乡人曾在黄竹岐乡东北面建有龙母庙，但县志对其规模和布局并没有详细记载。道光二十八年（1848），黄竹岐乡民在原先龙母庙庙址上建起了一间龙母古庙。龙母古庙自道光二十八年建成后，分别于咸丰八年（1858）及光绪十年（1884）先后两次重修。但重修的具体情况并未见诸文献资料，只在“龙母古庙”的石匾上留有重修日期的记载。可惜的是，有100多年历史、香火旺盛的黄岐龙母古庙在“文化大革命”期间被拆毁，仅留下了“龙母古庙”石牌匾。

20世纪80年代，改革开放后，港澳同胞担当起了龙母古庙重建大任，他们成立“黄竹岐历史文化研究会”，收集龙母古庙各种相关资料，发出重修倡议，筹集资金。1997年农历四月，龙母古庙得以重光。新龙母古庙位于旧龙母古庙西边，即岐阳古道西侧，占地近10亩（约6667平方米），同时原位于龙母古庙旁的观音庙、三娘庙也得以重建。

因为规划和资金问题，1997年重光的龙母古庙在布局和配套设施等方面存在不少问题。2008年黄岐龙母文化协会着手龙母古庙的修缮和扩建事宜，得到了当地政府和各界热心人士的支持。2011年11月，龙母古庙修缮扩建工程竣工，统称“龙母胜迹”。龙母胜迹沿袭古祠庙建筑风格，红墙、黄瓦、绿脊，重檐歇山式（古称九脊殿）或单檐歇山式建筑，地面、台阶、回廊、围栏均以白石砌嵌，部分还刻有龙纹，精致耐看。龙母胜迹由10个部分组成，包括正门、钟鼓楼、龟蛇池、许愿树、北帝殿、龙母古庙、龙床阁、三娘殿、观音殿、议事室，前后两进院落，加上门前公园，总面积近30亩（约20000平方米）。

民间相传黄岐龙母非常灵验，有什么事来黄岐龙母庙祈祷，龙母就会帮助人解困除厄。每年农历五月初八龙母诞辰当天，信众争相来到黄岐龙母庙膜拜龙母，乡亲们称为“乡例”。当天有信众虔诚参拜龙母、粤剧戏班连台演出、醒狮腾挪跳跃表演、庙前江上赛龙夺标，好不热闹。中华人民共和国成立前，龙母诞是黄岐一年一

the Daoguang period (1835) and printed in the 11th year of the Tongzhi period (1872) of the Qing Dynasty, the Dragon Mother Temple was located in "the northeast of Huangzhuqi", indicating that between the Wanli period and the 15th year of the Daoguang period, there was such a temple, but no detailed records of its scale and layout in the county chronicle. In the 28th year of the Daoguang period (1848) another Dragon Mother temple was built in the original site in Huangzhuqi. After that, it was renovated in the 8th year of Xianfeng period (1858) and the 10th year of the Guangxu period (1884) of the Qing Dynasty, but there were no records of the details except the dates of the renovations on the stone tablet "Dragon Mother Ancient Temple". It is a pity that the century-old temple was destroyed during the "Cultural Revolution", leaving only the stone tablet.

"龙母古庙"石匾
Stone Tablet of "Dragon Mother Ancient Temple"

In the 1980s, compatriots from Hong Kong and Macao initiated the reconstruction of the Dragon Mother Ancient Temple. By establishing the Huangzhuqi Historical and Cultural Research Association, they collected various relevant documents of the temple and issued a rebuilding initiative to raise funds. In the fourth lunar month of 1997, the Dragon Mother temple was reopened. The new temple is located to the west of the old one, that is, the west of Qiyang Ancient Path, occupying a floor area of about 6,667 square meters. At the same time, a Guanyin Hall and a Sanniang Hall have also been built next to it.

Due to planning and funding issues, the temple which was reopened in 1997 had many problems in layout and supporting facilities. In 2008, Huangqi Dragon Mother Cultural Association started the renovation and expansion of the temple, which were supported by the local government and people from all walks of life.

In November 2011, the renovation and expansion were completed. Collectively called the "Dragon Mother Scenery", the site adopts the traditional architectural style of temples, with red walls, yellow tiles, green ridges, and double-eaved hip-and-gable (called nine-ridge hall in ancient times) or single-eaved hip-and-gable buildings. The floor, steps, corridors, and fences are all built with white marble and some are even engraved with dragon patterns. The Dragon Mother Scenery consists of 10 parts, including the main entrance, the Bell and Drum Tower, the Turtle and Snake Pond, the Wishing Tree, the Hall of Emperor Xuanwu, the Dragon Mother Ancient Temple, the Dragon Bed Pavilion, the Sanniang Hall, the Guanyin Hall and a meeting room. With a front and a back courtyard and a park in front of the main entrance, the site covers a total area of about 20,000 square meters.

It is said that the Huangqi Dragon Mother is highly efficacious and can help people out of difficulties and bad luck if they come to pray in the temple. It has become a "village tradition" for people to worship her at the temple on her birthday. On this day, the disciples throng to the temple to show their piety, with incessant Cantonese Opera performances, lion dances, and dragon boat racing, rendering the occasion joyous and festive. Before 1949, the Birthday of the Dragon Mother was an important annual folk event in Huangqi.

After the founding of the People's Republic of China in 1949, the annual event was prohibited and all worshiping activities were abolished. Though there was a short recovery, it was short-lived. Since the 1980s, folk beliefs have gradually revived and the birthday activities have regained popularity, especially after the Huangqi Dragon Mother Temple was rebuilt, renovated and expanded in 1997, which provides both space and opportunities for the Dragon Mother Temple fair.

On the seventh day of the fifth lunar month in 2014, Huangqi held the first large-scale Dragon Mother worshiping activity, with grand and solemn ceremonies to show people's piety and respect for the Dragon Mother. The classic scene of "five dragons voyaging eastward to worship their mother" represents the dignity of the Dragon Mother and the filial piety of the dragon sons. On that day the "five dragon sons" came to Huangqi pier in five dragon boats in white,

度的民间盛会。

中华人民共和国成立后，神诞庙会一度被禁止，龙母祭祀活动也被废止，中间虽有短暂恢复，但也仅是昙花一现。20世纪80年代后，民间信仰逐渐复兴，神诞活动兴盛。尤其是1997年以后，黄岐龙母庙经过重建、修缮扩建，为龙母诞庙会的举办提供了空间和契机。

舞狮
Lion Dancing

2014年农历五月初七，黄岐举办了首届大型龙母诞拜祭活动，仪式隆重庄严，体现了人们对龙母的虔诚与尊崇。“五龙东渡探母”的经典场景，让人们体验到了龙母的威仪和龙子的孝德。活动当天，“五龙子”分别乘坐白、红、橙、蓝及绿色5艘龙舟，携带着罗伞、旗幡、锣鼓，一路戏水至黄岐码头登岸。“五龙子”甫登岸，一同拱手向龙母庙遥拜。随后在仪仗队的前呼后拥下，“五龙子”经过岐阳古道进入龙母庙拜祭龙母，一路上醒狮舞龙、鼓乐喧天，让夹道相迎的市民们大饱眼福。2015年“五龙子”一同乘坐一艘古色古香的游船东渡，一同登岸，寓意五龙子同气连枝，齐心携手，共同祭母。2017年，黄岐龙母诞入选佛山市非物质文化遗产名录。

广州昔日流传的民谣有“初一龙船起，初二龙船忍，初三初四游各地，初五龙船比，初七初八黄竹岐，初九初十龙船打崩鼻”，表明初七、初八龙母诞期间龙舟都聚集到黄竹岐。如今每年龙母诞，上午醒狮采青精彩纷呈，下午佛山南海、广州等地的数十艘龙舟都会齐聚黄岐参拜龙母，继而举行锦龙盛会。黄岐锦龙盛会形式多样，有彩龙巡游也有竞渡夺标，人们既可品味彩龙巡游的魅力，也可感受竞渡夺标的刺激。1981年，远近闻名的盐步老龙也打破了老龙不参拜龙母的惯例，首次来到黄岐参拜龙母，以后几乎每年都要来黄岐拜龙母，为龙母贺诞辰。但老龙不参加竞赛，只参加游龙，因此人们还可以欣赏到盐步老龙矫健、飘逸的风姿。

龙母胜迹
Dragon Mother Scenery

red, orange, blue and green, carrying special umbrellas, colored flags, drums and gongs and playing with water all the way. Once they arrived, they bowed to the Dragon Mother Temple in the distance. Then, escorted by the guard of honor, they entered the Dragon Mother Temple after passing the Qiyang Ancient Path. On the way, there were lion dances amid thunderous drumbeats. The scene was quite a feast for the eye. In 2015, the five dragon sons took the same ancient yacht east to land together, signifying that they were of the same heart and mind in worshiping their mother. In 2017, Huangqi Dragon Mother Birthday was included in Foshan's Intangible Cultural Heritage List.

A folk song circulated in Guangzhou says, "on the first day, the dragon boat is lifted; on the second, it endures; on the third and fourth, it travels around; on the fifth, it races; on the seventh and eighth, it goes to Huangzhuqi; and on the ninth and tenth, it contests vehemently." It indicates that on the seventh and eighth days of the fifth lunar month, dragon boats all gather in Huangzhuqi. In the morning of the Dragon Mother Birthday each year, dacing lions collect the greens; in the afternoon dozens of dragon boats from Nanhai of Foshan and from Guangzhou congregate in Huangqi to worship the Dragon Mother and attend the Dragon Boat Gala, which takes a variety of forms, including dragon boat pageants and races so that people can both enjoy the charisma of the former and the sensation of the latter. In 1981, the well-known Yanbu Old Dragon broke the tradition of not visiting the Dragon Mother and paid its first visit. Since then, it visits the Huangqi Dragon Mother almost every year to celebrate her birthday. But the Old Dragon does not take part in races, just cruises, so people can appreciate its vigorous and elegant demeanor.

4.5 Longyan Village in Leliu, a Sacred Place for Dotting the Dragon Eyes

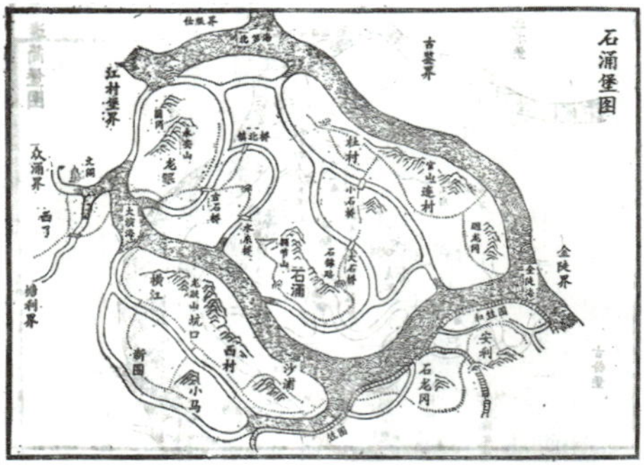

清代龙眼村地图
Map of Longyan Village in the Qing Dynasty

Located in Leliu Town, Shunde District of Foshan City, Longyan Village is a small water village. It was called Longzhu Village in ancient times and "zhu" means a piece of land surrounded by water in Chinese. There are two claims for the change in its name. One is that a multitude of longan (which is "longyan" in Chinese) trees are planted there, whereas the other is that the village has had the tradition of dotting the dragon eyes. There are several waterways, including Dayan, Longhua and Nanshui, and a ring creek surrounding the village. Naturally, boats have become a vital tool for production and transportation here. Given that, the ancestors of this village learned to use boats very early. With the population increase and economic growth, dragon boat activities have prospered.

It is said that in the Sui and Tang dynasties, it was very popular to build boats and hold boat activities to welcome the emperors' visits, so Longyan Village had its own dragon boats. In addition, a dragon boat col was built in front of the Xianggong Temple at the foot of the Yong'an Hill and Yuangang Hill for dragon

第五节　勒流龙眼　点睛圣地

龙眼村位于顺德勒流镇，是一个四面环水的小村落，古称龙渚，“渚”意为一小片水中陆地。龙渚后来改称龙眼，一说是因村中广植龙眼树，另一说是因村中有龙舟点睛的传统。龙眼村的水道有大演、龙华、南水等，有环村涌围绕村庄一周。四面环水，船是重要的生产和交通工具，因此龙眼村先民很早就学会使用船。随着人口繁衍、经济发展，龙眼村也兴起了龙舟之戏。

据说隋唐时期，民间盛行扎筏游龙，恭迎圣驾，龙眼村由此也有了龙船，村民们还在永安山圆岗山脚下的相公庙前修建龙船坳，接受周围龙船参拜。后来人们在此地筑围防洪，围名“同福”，龙船坳变作大塘，遂更名为“马石洲”，成为藏龙船之所。

明永乐年间，马石洲相公庙外开始有了龙舟点睛活动。明天顺年间，马石洲相公庙损毁，龙眼南

孖庙（左为太尉庙，右为华光庙）
Twin Temples (Left: Taiwei Temple, Right: Huaguang Temple)

约孖庙（华光庙、太尉庙）建成，龙舟点睛活动便改为在孖庙中的太尉庙举行。每逢节日，善男信女云集，上香祭拜。农历五月初三，顺德及周围龙舟都来到龙眼村孖庙，点睛祈福，热闹非凡。

人们认为，没有点睛的龙舟是“盲龙”，快速扒行会“插沙”（龙船翻沉后直冲河床插入沙中，除鼓手外的人和船会消失），所以龙舟要点睛，尤其是新龙舟必须点睛后才能下水。点了睛的龙舟，方可精神焕发，入水后平安顺利、不会翻沉、扒得飞快，赛龙才能夺冠。随着时间的推移，龙眼村逐渐成为顺德乃至珠三角地区的龙舟点睛的圣地。近年来，每年都有佛山顺德、南海，广州番禺、增城，中山、江门等地的龙舟到龙眼村举行点睛仪式，2015年龙眼村的“龙舟点睛”被评为广东省非物质文化遗产代表性项目。

龙眼村的龙舟点睛有着580多年的历史，逐渐形成了一整套独特的礼仪，包括祭拜、迎龙、抚龙、接龙、参拜、赠物、点睛、回龙、游龙、龙宴等仪式。

祭拜　农历四月三十日晚子时，村民进入太尉庙，敲打龙船鼓，燃香烛，放鞭炮，拜祭太尉周勃。接下来的日子里，村民们就开始做好点睛的准备工作，包括采买礼物、折龙船符、清理河涌、安排人手帮忙等。这几日，会陆续有龙舟来到龙眼村。

农历五月初三是龙舟点睛的日子，据说每年的这天必降雨，俗称“龙口水”。一大早，已经有善信们来太尉庙上香祭拜，庙内香烟缭绕。太尉庙内插着的帅旗已经整理好，罗伞、龙船鼓、铜锣等物已摆在太尉庙外。主持仪式的庙祝和长者们陆续来到庙中，恭候

boats from nearby villages to pay tribute. Afterwards, a fence named "Tongfu" (sharing happiness) was built here to prevent flood, so the col became a large pond to hide dragon boats and was renamed "Mashizhou".

The rite of dotting the dragon eyes outside the Xianggong Temple at Mashizhou can be traced back to the Yongle period (1403-1424) of the Ming Dynasty. When the temple was destroyed during the Tianshun period (1457-1464) of the Ming Dynasty, the twin temples of Huaguang Temple and Taiwei Temple were completed at Nanyue of the village. From then on, the eye dotting ceremony was held in the Taiwei Temple. On festive occasions, the temple is bustling with believers who come to burn incenses and worship, especially on the third day of the fifth lunar month when dragon boats from Shunde and nearby places all have their eyes dotted here to pray for blessings.

People believe that dragon boats without their eyes dotted are "blind dragons", so they will plunge into sand and everyone except the drummer and the boat will disappear. Therefore, it is important to dot the dragon eyes and especially those of new dragon boats before they enter the water.

Moreover, dragon boats with their eyes dotted are believed to be vigorous and energetic, so that they can have a safe journey without any accidents and move fast to win dragon boat races. As time goes by, Longyan Village has gradually become a sacred place for dragon boat eye dotting ceremonies in Shunde and even the whole Pearl River Delta. In recent years, dragon boats from Shunde and Nanhai of Foshan, Panyu and Zengcheng of Guangzhou, Zhongshan and Jiangmen have had their eyes dotted in Longyan Village. In 2015, the Dragon Boat Eye Dotting Ceremony of Longyan Village was listed as a representative item of the Intangible Cultural Heritage of Guangdong.

The eye dotting ceremony in Longyan Village has had a long history of more than 580 years and has formed a whole set of unique ceremonial procedures, which include making sacrifices, welcoming the dragon, caressing the dragon, ushering in the dragon, visiting the Taiwei(the supreme military officer in the government), exchanging gifts, dotting the eyes, reassembling the dragon, cruising around and having dragon boat meals.

Making Sacrifices At the eleventh hour in the evening of the 30th day of the fourth lunar month, villagers enter the Taiwei Temple, and worship Zhoubo, the Taiwei, by beating dragon boat drums, lighting incenses and candles and setting off firecrackers. In the next few days, villagers make preparations for the upcoming ceremony, such as purchasing gifts, making dragon boat amulets, cleaning the creek and allocating workload. In the meanwhile, dragon boats from other places keep coming to Longyan Village.

The third day of the fifth lunar month is the day to dot dragon eyes and according to legend, it is bound to rain and the rain is considered as the dragon's saliva. Early in the morning, the Taiwei Temple is crowded with disciples and covered with smokes from burning incenses and candles. Command flags are planted properly inside the temple whereas special umbrellas, drums and gongs are placed outside the temple. The temple attendant and the elders of the village who are to host the ceremony come to the temple early to wait for the dragon boats. About 200 meters away from the temple is a creek which is 3 or 4 meters wide, where 4 to 5 dragon boats can line up side by side at the same time. In 2014, an eye dotting platform made of stone slabs and a theme park featuring dragon boat eye dotting were built at the end of the creek.

Welcoming the Dragons Before 8 o'clock in the morning, a lot of people gather in the park and on the river banks, looking forward to seeing the dragon boats, and several villagers are already waiting at the eye dotting platform to welcome them. People get excited on hearing the drumbeats of approaching dragon boats. When the boats turn into the small creek, the crowds start cheering and setting off firecrackers.

Caressing the Dragons Afterwards, dragon boats line up in the creek, waiting for the carefully chosen time to have their eyes dotted. When the auspicious moment comes, all dragon boats pull up to the shore and the paddlers take off the dragon head and tail and the dragon card. As a rule, the dragon head goes first, followed by the card and then the tail, symbolizing good order and completeness. The moment dragon heads go ashore they are surrounded by women and their kids. People caress the dragon heads, beards, horns and tails because it is believed that touching the dragon head can bring wealth and longevity while the tail good fortune throughout the year.

来自四面八方的群龙前来祭拜点睛。距离太尉庙200米左右有一条河涌，河阔三四米，可并排停泊四五艘龙船。河涌尽头是石板铺就的点睛台和绿树成荫的龙舟点睛主题公园，均为2014年修葺。

迎龙 早上八点钟不到，公园内、河涌边已经聚集了不少人，人们翘首以盼，等待来点睛的龙舟。点睛台已经安排了几位村民守候在此，准备迎接来参拜的龙舟。当隐隐约约的龙船鼓声传来，人群开始骚动，龙舟拐弯进入小河涌时，河涌边的人们欢呼起来，接待的村民迅速点燃早已准备好的鞭炮，欢迎来参拜的龙舟。

抚龙 龙舟陆续抵达点睛台，并排停泊在河涌中，等待点睛吉时的到来。吉时一到，龙舟靠岸，扒丁们卸下龙头、龙尾和龙牌。按规矩龙头先行，龙牌在中，龙尾押后，寓意前后有序，完整无缺。龙头甫一上岸，许多妇女便拖儿带女围住龙头，大家抚摸龙头、龙须、龙角、龙尾，寓意“摸龙头，富贵添寿；摸龙尾，一年好到尾”。

接龙 扒丁们抬着龙头、龙尾，来到太尉庙前，太尉庙外鞭炮齐鸣，庙内锣鼓喧天，一直不停歇，门口还有醒狮起舞迎接。来点睛的每一艘龙舟都会派一位长者将龙船帖和龙船符（通常用红色袋子装着）一起交给太尉庙门边接待的长者。长

扒丁抬着龙头进入太尉庙
Paddlers Carrying the Dragon Head into Taiwei Temple

者会记下每艘来访龙舟的龙船牌信息，登记到访龙舟的数量，以方便后续的结算。

参拜 抬龙头的人踏进庙门就会说吉利话，如“万事胜意”“龙马精神”等。在庙中长者的指点下，龙头正向太尉像摆放，龙牌放在中间，龙尾放在最后，扒丁一起参拜太尉。

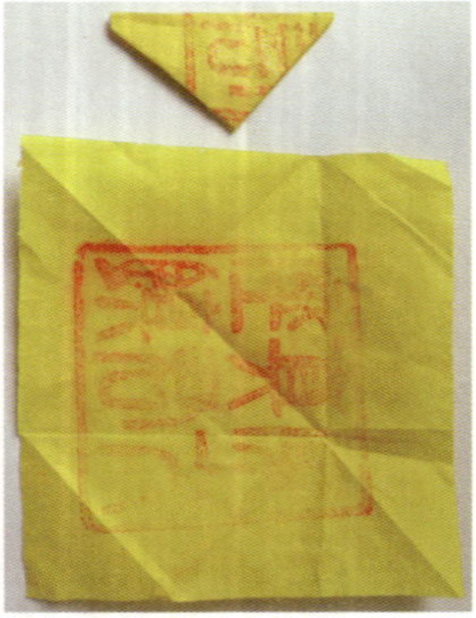

龙符
Dragon Amulets

赠物 参拜完毕，一旁的长者就往龙口塞龙眼叶、黄皮叶，同时说着“身体健康”“龙马精神”等吉利话。龙舟扒丁会送上利市和龙船符，利市钱也就一二十元，主要是为了吉利。长者们又回赠礼物，包括利市一封、米酒两瓶、饼干一包、鲜果数对。

点睛 龙眼村的点睛人固定为太尉庙庙祝或其传人，目前龙眼村的点睛仪式主持人是梁汉勇，他从2007年开始主持点睛仪式，已经主持了10多年，对龙舟点睛的仪式和程序非常熟悉。相互赠物后，梁汉勇拿起毛笔蘸上朱砂，一边喊着“龙腾虎跃”“风调雨顺”“身体健康”“龙马精神”等吉祥语，一边点睛，旁边的扒丁则大声呼应“好嘢”。点完龙眼，还要依顺序在龙牌龙尾各处点数笔，寓意年头顺到年尾。据梁汉勇透露，点睛时笔锋必须朝上，寓意步步高升、奋发向上。点睛仪式完毕，“龙”不得沿原路回去，而是要顺时针绕庙行一周，俗称“行大运”。龙舟先进入后殿拜祭观音娘娘，后拜祭右侧庙宇中供奉的华光大帝，再

Ushering in the Dragons When paddlers carry the dragon head and tail to the front of the temple, firecrackers are set off outside while drums and gongs are beaten constantly inside and lion dances are performed to greet them at the gate. Later on, each dragon boat sends an elder to present the visiting card and amulet (usually packed in red packages) to another elder at the gate, who then writes down the name of each visiting dragon boat and counts the number for future use.

Worshiping the Taiwei On entering the Taiwei Temple, people carrying the dragon heads express blessings like "All as you wish" and "Full of vigor and vitality". Under the guidance of the elders in the temple, the dragon heads are placed in the front, facing the Taiwei's statue, the cards in the middle and the tails at the back. Then all the paddlers worship the Taiwei together.

Exchanging Gifts After worshiping the Taiwei, the elders standing aside put leaves of longan and wampee into the dragon mouths and say auspicious words like "May you be in good health" and "Full of vigor and vitality" in the meantime. Then paddlers give some lucky money in a red envelope and dragon boat amulets to the elders. The amount is just RMB 10 or 20 for it is only a ceremonial procedure. In return, the elders give the paddlers some lucky money in a red envelope, two bottles of rice wine, a packet of cookies and some pairs of fresh fruits.

点睛
Dotting the Eyes

Dotting the Dragon Eyes In Longyan Village, only the temple attendants and their successors are eligible to dot the dragon eyes. The current attendant is called Liang Hanyong who has done the job since 2007. With more than 10 years of experience, he knows every step of the ritual inside and out.

After exchanging gifts, Liang inks his

writing brush with cinnabar to dot the dragon eyes while saying some auspicious words like "Dragons rise and tigers leap Wind and rain come in their time" "Good health and Full of vigor and vitality". While he is so doing, paddlers respond with cheers. Liang then draws several lines on the card and tail in order, representing the wish that everything will go smoothly throughout the year. According to Liang, the writing brush must move upward, meaning to get promotion and move upward. After the ceremony, the dragon boats cannot return by the same route but go around the temple clockwise as a way of praying for good luck. The dragon boats first pay tribute to Guanyin at the back of the temple and then Emperor Huaguang in the Huaguang Temple on the right. After that, the dragon boats leave the Huaguang Temple and return to the creek.

Reassembling the Dragons After the dragon heads, tails and cards are reassembled onto the dragon boats moored in the creek, all paddlers go on board, taking their positions and getting ready to start the dragon boat cruise.

Cruising Around Paddlers row the dragon boats along the ring creek and receive gifts and blessings from the villagers, who present gifts at several "gift spots" to the dragon boats coming from afar to show their generosity and hospitality. When passing each spot, the dragon boats receive gifts and lucky money and give their visiting card and dragon boat amulet in return. During the tour, paddlers perform various techniques, such as turning the dragon head around, shaking the dragon head and tail, turning the special umbrellas, and waving the colorful flags. They even splash water to each other for fun. In recent years, The organizers in Leliu have also added some other unique cultural activities to the dragon boat cruise, including *Piaose*(flying dance of children dressed in ancient costumes) of Zhongchong Village, and one-person dragon boats and lion boats of Huanglian, Longyan. In addition, several projects of Shunde's intangible cultural heritage such as octave drums and gongs as well as dragon boat talking and singing have been introduced to Longyan Village and received warm welcome from villagers and visitors.

Having Dragon Boat Meals Dragon boat meals used to be simple in Longyan Village. Each dragon boat brought two or three dishes along and after the eye dotting ceremony, the paddlers had their meals on the ground. Nowadays,

从华光庙出门上路返回河涌。

回龙　龙舟的龙头、龙尾及龙牌返回河涌中龙舟停泊处，并旋即归位，扒丁们全部上船各就各位，准备游龙。

游龙　龙舟扒到环村涌中，绕行龙眼村一周，接受龙眼村人的礼物和祝福。龙眼村人对远道而来的龙舟非常慷慨热情，村里沿河设置了数个“赠礼点”，游龙过程中，每个赠礼点都会派送礼物和利市，龙舟就回赠龙船帖和龙船符。各龙舟在河涌中游得兴奋，将自己的各种绝技展示出来，转龙头、颠龙头龙尾、转罗伞、甩彩旗，还互相泼水嬉戏，好不热闹。近年来，勒流街道还把众涌水上飘色、龙眼黄连龙虱和狮子船等特色文化搬到河涌中巡游，顺德非遗项目锣鼓柜、龙舟说唱也来到龙眼村开演，受到了村民和游客的欢迎。

龙眼村的赠礼点
Gifts Delivery Site of Longyan Village

龙宴　龙宴就是吃龙舟饭，以前龙眼村的龙舟饭非常简单，都是龙舟自己带来的，菜式只有两三个，点睛仪式结束后，扒丁们就会找个空地蹲下来吃龙舟饭。现在龙眼村的龙舟饭不再是龙舟自带了，村中会请流动餐馆上门烹饪宴席，有需要的就会预订数桌。菜式也很丰富，均安烧猪、龙眼油煮粽、龙眼炸猪肉等顺德美食和龙眼特色菜让人食欲大增。

前几年，来点睛的龙舟不多，近两年来点睛的龙舟越来越多，2017年有90多艘。让龙眼村人惊喜的是，近年前来点睛的龙舟扒丁越来越年轻，相比一二十年前以四五十岁的中年人为主，现在则以二三十岁的青年人为主力。年轻人越来越多地参与龙舟点睛等龙舟活动，让我们看到了更多龙舟文化传承的希望。

dragon boats do not take their own meals along anymore. Instead, mobile restaurants are hired to cook for them and they can order whatever they like. In addition, various dishes are served for people to feast on, including local specialties such as Jun'an Roast Pig, Longyan Boiled Zongzi, and Longyan Fried Pork.

The past few years have witnessed an increase in the number of dragon boats attending the eye dotting ceremony in Longyan Village. In 2017, there were more than 90 dragon boats. To the delight of the villagers, more and more younger people participate in this event. Ten to twenty years ago, most paddlers were people over 40 or 50. Today, young people in their twenties or thirties become the primary force instead. This increasing engagement of younger people in dragon boat activities conveys the hope of inheriting the dragon boat culture.

4.6 Hometown of Five-People Dragon Boats Renowned for its Songs

Baini Town is a typical water town in Lingnan, and the south gate of Sanshui, The town is crisscrossed by water networks and fish ponds with 53% of it covered in water. Its unique water culture and geographical environment have nurtured its time-honored dragon boat culture and its people's love for dragon boats.

There is a legend about the origin of dragon boat racing in Baini. Protected by the Xijiang Dragon King, the Baini people enjoyed good weather and a comfortable life. Later, because of his merits in protecting the people, the Xijiang

激烈的龙舟赛（白坭文化站）
Fierce Dragon Boat Race (Baini Township Cultural Station)

第六节 五人龙舟之乡 龙舟歌标传扬

白坭镇为典型的岭南水乡，是三水的南大门。全镇水体面积约占53%，水网纵横交错，鱼塘星罗棋布，独特的水乡文化和地理环境孕育了白坭源远流长的龙舟文化和白坭人的龙舟情怀。

关于白坭赛龙习俗的源起有一个传说：因西江龙王的庇佑，白坭风调雨顺，百姓安居乐业。后来西江龙王因护民守土有功，被传召至天宫提拔重用。为了表达对西江龙王的感谢与不舍，百姓划着各种船只相送，后来就逐渐演化成赛龙舟的习俗。这虽然是传说，但反映了白坭人对龙的崇拜和对划龙舟的热爱。据说龙舟赛事远在明清时期就深受白坭人青睐，五人龙舟、十一人龙舟和二十三人龙舟等至今仍是许多村组的传村之宝。尤其是五人龙舟竞赛活动在当地广受欢迎，并传承至今。民间认为五人龙舟是由以前运输粮食的禾艇演变而来——白坭是三水区的主要粮食产区，大片稻田又被河涌分割开来，因此小巧方便的禾艇成为农忙时节运输粮食的重要工具。农闲时节，人们就会划着这种小船竞赛娱乐，由此五人龙舟赛逐渐成为白坭人最主要的端午节日民俗。

白坭赛龙历史悠久，村民对龙舟情有独钟，白坭大多数村落都拥有数艘龙舟。白坭龙舟以五人龙舟为主，据不完全统计，截至

2018年，全镇拥有五人龙舟200余艘，十一人龙舟和五十人龙舟共100多艘。2018年12月，三水白坭镇获评为“广东省五人龙舟特色镇”。白坭五人龙舟以杉木打造，尖头、细腰、窄尾，整个船身显得很修长。与佛山各地的传统龙比较，白坭五人龙舟没有任何装饰，无龙头、龙尾、锣鼓、幡旗等，去掉了这些装饰的白坭五人龙舟非常轻巧，速度也极快。赛龙时，一艘艘尖头窄尾、颜色鲜艳的五人龙舟在水面上迅疾如飞，非常刺激。

白坭龙舟活动的程序和礼仪与佛山其他地方稍有差别，主要有旺龙、赛龙、散标、藏龙等几个环节。旺龙也称“祭龙”，在下水前选定一个吉日吉时举行仪式，地点可以是存放龙舟的会所、祠堂或者参赛龙舟入水的岸边。旺龙前夕，村中好福气的妇女会一起购买香烛、祭品等，做好祭祀的准备。然后人们将龙舟抬出来平放在地上，由赛龙扒丁主持仪式，香火点燃后插在龙舟旁边，同时还要燃放鞭炮，扒丁们虔诚拜祭神灵北帝、洪圣大王等，祈求赛龙得胜、顺利平安。其他的村民也会过来观看仪式，为扒丁们加油鼓劲。举办旺龙仪式，既是为了讨个“好意头”，祈福祛灾，又是为了提振士气，提醒大家好好训练，争取赛龙取得好成绩。由此，白坭龙舟活动拉开了序幕。此后，三三两两的龙舟就出现在江河或水库中，加紧训练。

白坭赛龙采取马拉松式的“一长九短”十圈赛制，赛程视规模大小从10多千米到40多千米不等，主要有五关，即放龙、破浪、转洞、劈龙门、休标。白坭放龙采取的是传统的“舵手放龙”，礼炮一响，站成一排直线的舵手就会急速向着自己的船只飞奔，瞬间数

Dragon King was promoted to Heaven. In order to show their gratitude and attachment to him, people rowed various boats to bid farewell, which later evolved into the custom of dragon boat racing. This legend reflects Baini people's worship of the dragon and their love for dragon boating. It is said that dragon boat racing was popular among the Baini people as early as the Ming and Qing dynasties. The five-people, eleven-people and twenty-three people dragon boats are still treasures of many villages, among which races with the five-people ones are especially popular. It is believed that the five-people dragon boats had evolved from the rice-carrying boats. Baini is a major rice production zone of Sanshui District, where paddies are divided by creeks, so the small and convenient rice-carrying boats are major means of transport in the harvest seasons. In the off seasons, people race with this kind of boats for entertainment. Gradually the five-people dragon boat racing has become the most important folk custom of the Dragon Boat Festival in Baini.

Dragon boat racing in Baini has a long history and is well liked by the villagers. Most Baini villages have several dragon boats, which are mainly five-people ones. According to incomplete statistics, as of 2018, there were over 200 five-people dragon boats, and more than 100 eleven-people and fifty-people ones in Baini Town. In December 2018, Baini Town was awarded the title "Characteristic Town of Five-People Dragon Boats of Guangdong Province". Baini five-people dragon boats are made of China fir, with a pointed head, a thin hull and a narrow tail, so the whole boat looks slender. Compared with traditional dragon

三水五人龙舟
Five-People Dragon Boat of Sanshui

boats in other places of Foshan, Baini five-people ones have no decorations, not even a head, a tail, a drum, a gong or a flag. As a result, the boats are light and fast. In racing, these colorful boats dash through the water like flying.

The procedures and rituals of Baini dragon boat activities are slightly different from those of other places in Foshan. They mainly include worshiping the dragon, racing the dragon, dispersing the trophies, and hiding the dragon. To worship the dragon, an auspicious time and day must be chosen before a dragon boat enters the water. It can be done at the clubhouse or the ancestral hall where the dragon boat is stored or on the bank where it is to enter the water. On the eve of the worship day, the blessed women in the village buy incenses and candles and make preparations for the worship. Then the dragon boat is laid flat on the ground. The paddlers will start the worshiping ceremony, burning incenses and candles and placing them by the dragon boat. At the same time, they set off firecrackers and worship Emperor Xuanwu and King Hongsheng, praying for safety and victory in racing. Other villagers also come to watch the ceremony and cheer for the paddlers. The purposes of the worshiping ceremony are not only to wish for good luck but also to boost the morale of the paddlers. It reminds them to practice hard to win good results in the coming races. The worshiping ceremony unveils the dragon boat activities of Baini. After that, a number of dragon boats start their training in rivers or reservoirs.

Baini dragon boat racing adopts a ten-round Marathon style, including one long round and nine short ones. The length varies from just over 10 km to over 40 km depending on the scale of racing. There are five phases in a race, including releasing the dragon, breaking the waves, turning around, knocking at the dragon gate and competing for the trophies. In Baini, the dragons are traditionally released by the helmsmen. At the sound of the saluting gun, the helmsmen, who are standing in a line, rush out to their respective dragon boats. Instantly, dozens or even over a hundred men are sprinting on the beach, while the spectators are shouting and cheering for them. Breaking the waves means that the dragon boats are moving fast on water. Turning around means that the dragon boats turn back after reaching a certain point. According to the rules, passing the point once means completing one round. The racing is a long

十上百个壮汉在沙滩上疾跑，岸上观者呐喊加油声此起彼伏，现场一下子沸腾起来了。破浪是指龙舟在水中乘风破浪、疾驰而过。转洞即经过折返点折返——白坭采取绕圈竞速赛形式，转过折返点一次返回起点算一圈。这个过程比较漫长，要持续两个多小时甚至更长时间，而且白坭赛龙大多是在下午太阳最烈的时候开始，对扒丁的体力和耐力是一个极大的考验。紧张刺激的放龙过后，漫长的绕圈竞速的精彩度大大降低，岸边观众情绪不免懈怠下来，但一些大妈大婶们真是龙舟的忠实拥趸，她们的呐喊加油声一直没有停歇，一场赛事下来，声音嘶哑、嗓子冒烟的大有人在。赛道边一些男子泡在水中，手中端着盘子，为扒丁们递水送粥补充体能。烈日下的他们静静地站在齐胸部的水中，极大地鼓舞了疲惫的扒丁们。龙舟在规定水域内扒到规定趟数的最后一趟，先抵者过龙门时，高举龙桡独劈龙门，以示捷足先得，谓之劈龙门。最后一趟是休标阶段，即争夺锦标（高标）的阶段。放龙和休标，分别标志着整个龙舟赛的开端和结束，也是全赛程中最精彩的环节。

劈龙门（白坭文化站）
Knocking at the Dragon Gate (Baini Township Cultural Station)

白坭的标部还是传统的高标、罗伞、烧猪、美酒。高标用红、橙、黄、绿等各色布匹裁成，宽约88厘米，高约8.8米，赛龙当日

高标罗伞（白坭文化站）
Gaobiao and Special Umbrellas (Baini Township Cultural Station)

用竹竿挑着竖立在标埠，上面贴着用红纸写成的四字成语，“独占鳌头”表示第一名，“双龙出海”表示第二名。

龙舟赛结束，就是散标。龙舟赛中夺得高标的龙舟队伍，在本村聚餐吃散标饭来庆祝，同时对赢得的高标、奖品等进行竞拍，将宴会的气氛推向高潮。

白坭的龙舟主要为杉木龙舟，藏在祠堂、会所等室内。五人龙舟、十一人龙舟没有龙头、龙尾，就整艘放在室内。长龙要把龙头、龙尾拆下来，和龙身分开收藏，等待来年的龙舟节来临。

白坭龙舟文化的兴盛，与龙舟歌标的传播密切相关。龙舟歌标流行于南海、顺德、三水等地，在三水北部地方叫“龙船引”，而在白坭金本、西樵民乐一带叫“歌标”。关于龙舟歌标的形式、内容、发展、作用、发展历史与现状等内容前文已有介绍，此处不再赘述。

在三水白坭，除了徐国林，还有几位会写作龙舟歌标的老人，如陈玉昆、朱伟洪等，他们都是土生土长的白坭人。如今，三水白坭镇着力打造“广东省五人龙舟之乡”，有计划把龙舟歌标的传承

process, lasting for over two hours or even longer. As the races usually take place in the afternoon when the sun is the strongest, it is an ordeal for the paddlers' stamina. After the excitement of releasing the dragons, the long process of round-trip racing is not as spectacular, so the enthusiasm of the audience may wane, but some middle-aged ladies are really great fans of dragon boats, cheering all the time. After the races, a lot of them have got a sore throat. Some strong men are standing in the chest-deep water by the racing course in the blazing sun for hours, holding plates on which there is porridge and water for the tired paddlers to refresh themselves. When a dragon boat comes to the last round and arrives at the dragon gate first, it will knock at it with a paddle to signal its lead, so the act is called "knocking at the dragon gate". The last round of rowing is also the phase of competing for the trophies. Releasing the dragon and competing for the trophies respectively mark the beginning and end of the dragon boat racing, and are the most interesting parts in the whole process.

Baini trophies are traditional *Gaobiao*, special umbrellas, roast pigs and wine. The *Gaobiao* are cut from red, orange, yellow and green cloth. They are about 88 centimeters wide and 8.8 meters high. On the racing day, they are erected on bamboo poles. On the *Gaobiao* are some Chinese characters on red paper indicating the first or second place.

Following the race is dispersing the trophies. The dragon boat teams that have won the *Gaobiao* have the meal together in the village to celebrate their victory and offer their *Gaobiao* and prizes for a bid, which become highlight of the gathering.

Baini dragon boats, which are mainly made of China fir, are stored in ancestral halls or clubhouses. The five-people and eleven-people dragon boats have no heads or tails, so the whole boats are stored indoors. For longer dragons, the head and the tail have to be removed and stored separately from the body until the next Dragon Boat Festival.

The prosperity of Baini dragon boat culture is closely related to the spread of dragon boat songs, which are popular in places such as Nanhai, Shunde and Sanshui. They are given different names in different places of Foshan.

In Baini, Sanshui, apart from Xu Guolin, there are some other seniors capable of writing dragon boat songs, such as Chen Yukun and Zhu Weihong. All of them are locals of Baini. Now that Baini Town tries to establish itself as a "Hometown of Five-People Dragon Boats in Guangdong Province", it plans to put the inheritance of dragon boat songs on the agenda, so that this distinctive folk culture can be further developed.

Xu Guolin, born in the mid-1930s, has loved classical literature since childhood, especially poems with strict meters. When he was young, before the dragon boat races, dragon boat songs were pasted in the villages. Those rhythmic songs were Xu's favorite reading materials. He would read them aloud and even recite them. He can still recall the dragon boat songs that he had read in his childhood. After he had grown up, he started writing dragon boat songs, couplets, and poems for ribbon-cutting events. Since the 1980s, he has created over 30 dragon boat songs for villages or various institutions.

Xu says it is not easy to write dragon boat songs. The more he writes, the more difficult he feels. For one thing, it is hard to innovate in sentence structure and language, because dragon boat songs need to follow the same rhyme in all sentences, but cannot use the same or similar words repetitively. For another thing, it is hard to integrate national events, current affairs in politics and development in society into the songs. In order to create some dragon boat songs that are both rhythmic and representative of Sanshui characteristics, Xu keeps the habit of chanting various classical literary works including poems and songs and taking notes. At the same time, he studies various government reports and documents and tries to express them in succinct and rhythmic language. The song he wrote for the Hengfu Cup National Day Dragon Boat Invitation Tournament of Sanshui District, Foshan City in 2015 includes four parts: introduction to the dragon

本书作者采访徐国林老师
Author of This Book Interviewing Mr. Xu Guolin

龙舟说唱
Dragon Boat Talking and Singing

工作提上日程，让这一极具本土特色的民间文化得以延续发展。

徐国林生于20世纪30年代中期，自幼爱好古典文学，尤其是格律严整的古典诗词。龙舟赛事前在四乡贴出的富有古典诗词韵律美感的歌标是徐国林儿时最喜爱的文学读物，他会反复诵读直至背诵下来，幼时看过的歌标他到现在还能脱口而出。徐国林成年后开始创作歌标、对联、剪彩文字等。20世纪80年代开始，陆续有村落或单位请他创作歌标，近30年来他共创作了30多首歌标。

徐国林说写作歌标并非易事，尤其是现在越写越难，一方面难在句式和语言的创新，因为歌标需要“一韵到底”，但又不能反复运用相似的词句；另一方面难在如何更好地将国家大事、时事政治、社会发展等写进歌标。为了创作出既有韵律美感，又能反映三水特色的龙舟歌标，徐国林一直坚持诵读各种古典文学著作，包括诗词歌赋，并用心记下读书笔记，同时研读大量政府工作报告、文件等，并用简洁、押韵的文字表达出来。徐国林撰写的2015年佛山市三水区“恒福杯”国庆龙舟邀请赛歌标包括了四个部分，即“赛龙起引”“中华崛起”“三水崛起”“竞渡歌谣”，有1300多字，是长篇歌标的典范。“赛龙起引”为一首七言诗，“国庆迎来恒福杯，龙舟大赛鼓频催。捧猪扛酒君休笑，夺锦称雄奏凯回”，格律严整。“中华崛起”部分则从回忆中国近代史开端，对中国近现代100多年的屈辱史和中华人民共和国成立后取得的成就进行了描述。“三水崛起”部分详尽概括了三水近年来的经济、商业、交通、党建、民生等各方面的成就，可见徐国林在创作之前下足了功夫。“竞渡歌谣”部分详列了参加比赛的注意事项、比赛规程、观赛地点、比赛现场情形、奖励名次和奖品等，读完让人对比赛了然于胸。

boat racing, “rejuvenation of the Chinese nation”, “rejuvenation of Sanshui”, and the dragon boat racing ballad, with a total of over 1, 300 Chinese characters, an exemplar of long dragon boat songs. The introduction to the dragon boat racing is a poem of four lines, each containing seven characters, which is composed with strict meters. The part of “rejuvenation of the Chinese nation” describes how China has emerged from the humiliation that lasted over a century and what achievements it has made since the founding of the People’s Republic of China in 1949. The part of “rejuvenation of Sanshui” summarizes Sanshui’s achievements in recent years in terms of economy, commerce, transportation, the party building, people’s livelihood and others, all of which show that Xu had done a lot of thinking and research before composing the song. The racing ballad lists the detailed information about the precautions, racing rules, venues, racing scenes, rewarding rules and prizes.

食海鲜
饮粤宴
佛山市政府
推荐接待用酒
业融合，打造优质文化品牌。
庆